STRUCTURAL FABULATION

UNIVERSITY OF NOTRE DAME

WARD-PHILLIPS LECTURES IN

ENGLISH LANGUAGE AND LITERATURE

Volume 7

Structural Fabulation

An Essay on Fiction
of the Future

ROBERT SCHOLES

Notre Dame & London

UNIVERSITY OF NOTRE DAME PRESS

PR
830
S35
S3

Copyright © 1975 by
University of Notre Dame Press
Notre Dame, Indiana 46556

Library of Congress Cataloging in Publication Data

Scholes, Robert E
   Structural fabulation.

   (Ward-Phillips lectures in English language and
literature ; v. 7)
   Based on 4 lectures delivered at the University of
Notre Dame in 1974, now extensively revised.
   Bibliography: p.
   Includes index.
   1. Science fiction, English—History and criticism—
Addresses, essays, lectures. 2. Science fiction,
American—History and criticism—Addresses, essays,
lectures. 3. English fiction—20th century—History
and criticism—Addresses, essays, lectures. 4. Ameri-
can fiction—20th century—History and criticism—
Addresses, essays, lectures. I. Title. II. Series.
PR830.S35S3   823'.0876   74-30167
ISBN 0-268-00570-2
ISBN 0-268-00571-0 pbk.

Manufactured in the United States of America

For Chris, Peter, Cindy, Ric, Greg, Mike—the Future

Contents

FOREWORD   ix

1 The Fictional Criticism of the Future   1

2 The Roots of Science Fiction   27

3 Structural Fabulation   45

4 The Good Witch of the West   77

AFTERWORD   101

    Select Bibliography   105

    Index   109

Foreword

THE FOUR LECTURES THAT CONSTITUTE THIS essay in criticism are intended as a kind of prolegomena to the serious reading of what we loosely call "science fiction." In the first lecture I consider the contemporary situation of fiction and its attendant literary criticism, arguing a case for fiction that concerns itself with the future. This lecture is polemical—some would say too much so. The second lecture is more speculative, offering both a generic theory and a historical framework in which to consider contemporary works of fiction that insist on some radical discontinuity between the worlds they present to us and the world of our experience. Both the first two lectures are general and theoretical in their emphases. The last two are more specific and practical. The third presents a perspective on the varieties of modern SF, through a discussion of certain borderline or extreme cases. The last lecture focusses on one contemporary writer whose work will stand the most rigorous critical examination and, indeed, profit from it.

All four of these talks were written for and first delivered at the University of Notre Dame as the Ward-Phillips lectures for 1974. I am grateful to Notre Dame for continuing the humane tradition of these lectures and for allowing me to consider a subject so "popular" and "contemporary" in such an august series of presentations. The lectures have been revised extensively as a result of their presentation and discussion at Notre Dame, and their re-presentation at the University of Iowa. I have not met all valid objections, I know, but I have tried at least to clarify my own objectionable positions to enable a useful dialogue in the future. Among those offering significant criticisms I remember most vividly Patrick Callahan, Edward Vasta, Gerald Bruns, David Chamberlain, John Gerber, Carl Klaus, Larry Martin, Michael Ryan, and Thomas Whitaker. I can offer them thanks, if not satisfaction, here. A few pages of the first lecture have been retained from a talk on "Stillborn Literature," given at the meeting of the Midwest Modern Language Association in 1973 and published in the 1974 *Bulletin* of that organization. A revised version, much closer to the present text has appeared in the *TriQuarterly*. And a version of the fourth lecture appeared in the *Hollins Critic* of April 1974. I am grateful to the editors of these journals for permission to recycle these materials in the present book.

For those who know my earlier studies in fiction, this volume, slim as it is, may be seen to continue and develop ideas elaborated elsewhere. It is a companion piece to my earlier essays on contemporary fiction and metafiction, which appeared in *The Fabulators* and various literary magazines. And it rests upon the theoretical foundations of my studies in *The Nature of Narrative* and *Structuralism in Literature.* But it is, finally, an essay not a treatise, a series of lectures on a single topic, not an exhaustive investigation of that topic. For the student who wants to go beyond what is provided here, I offer some suggestions in the bibliography, where the reader unfamiliar with the basic texts of contemporary science fiction will find a short list of works that according to various criteria have been accounted excellent.

1

The Fictional Criticism

of the Future

KNOWING ONE THING IS A WAY OF NOT KNOWING something else. If I know the earth is flat, this is a way of not knowing that it is round. Frequently— usually—knowing something easy is a way of not knowing something hard. With this in mind, I wish to discuss some of the things we know about fiction and criticism—and perhaps to hint at what they prevent us from knowing.

Once we knew that fiction was about life and criticism was about fiction—and everything was simple. Now we know that fiction is about other fiction, is criticism in fact, or metafiction. And we know that criticism is about the impossibility of anything being about life, really, or even about fiction, or, finally, about anything. Criticism has taken the very idea of "aboutness" away from us. It has taught us that language is tautological, if it is not nonsense, and to the extent that it is about anything it is about itself. Mathematics is about mathematics, poetry is about poetry, and criticism is about the impossibility of its own existence.

That this hard won position should prove untenable is not simply a fault in our critical guides. Having reached such a peak of solipsism is, like climbing Mount Everest, a genuine achievement. But having climbed Everest one's choices are limited. One can remain at the peak and perish of inanity; one can fall or jump off; or try to climb down again. The great trick is to climb down by a different route, and thus see the world in another way. One climbs Everest for the sake of the new perspectives brought back from the peak. My intent in this essay is to put the present situation of fiction and the criticism of fiction in such a new perspective. For I, too, have been to the peak or near it.

Most of our writers and critics of fiction at the present time can be divided into two major groups, which operate on rather different principles. I shall return later on to consider more elaborately the nature of these groups—and some others—and the relationships among them but for the moment they may be characterized in terms of the metaphor already developed here. One group has been to the peak, the other has not. The latter group is handicapped by its faith in an outworn creed. The former is also handicapped, but by its loss of faith, its doubt about the very possibilities of fiction at the present time. My primary concern is with this group, because I believe that its experience of doubt, the intellectual vertigo that assails all those who look deep into the verbal abyss, is an absolutely necessary experience for the writer in our time. To move, to change, even to continue, we must go through this place. There is no way around it. My faith in the necessity of doubt puts me in a doubly paradoxical position. I must urge some to approach the abyss for the first time, even as I exhort others to pass beyond it. For both of these tasks to be accomplished, it will be necessary to consider in less metaphorical terms the nature of the verbal abyss itself, before trying to suggest what may lie on the other side of it.

The philosophical anguish I am concerned with here should not be confused with what some take to be the unique horror of modern existence, though many students of literature may seek to blame artistic difficulties on existential problems. Frankly, I know of no scale in which to balance the horror of modern life against that of any other age, and I am convinced that every age has had its share of horrors for those sensitive enough to register them. No, the vision I am concerned with here is a merely verbal one, as the vision of a mystic may be considered to be merely spiritual.

Put simply, contemporary writers and critics have lost faith in the ability of language to correspond with the non-verbal parts of life. This was, most emphatically, not a problem felt by the great writers of the early twentieth century. Joyce and

Proust, for instance, shared a faith in the ability of their verbal art to give coherence to the actualities of the world around them, however much they sensed the inadequacies of traditional "realism." But modern critics (like Roland Barthes in *S/Z*) have shown with devastating irony that even a great "realist" like Balzac did not make his linguistic code correspond with reality in-itself, but simply alluded in his language to other already codified beliefs, other codes which themselves inevitably lack genuine ontological status. Language is language and reality is reality—and never the twain shall meet. Thus say the Kiplings of the new epistemology, nor can we dismiss this intellectual apartheid as mere literary jingoism, for the physicists are quite ready to admit the same shortcomings in their mathematical language. All systems of notation offer us models of reality rather than descriptions of it. Nor is the way out of this dilemma to be found by denying its existence. The fiction of the future and the criticism of the future must find a way to accept this situation and continue functioning so as to be useful to mankind.

Here I must digress a bit in order to discuss the uses of fiction in general, before considering the way these uses relate to the present situation and the future. Fiction has always been characterized by its ability to perform two functions. Some fictions accomplish both equally, some emphasize one; but a work which accomplishes neither must be a bad fiction or no fiction at all. We may call

4

these two functions *sublimation* and *cognition.* As sublimation, fiction is a way of turning our concerns into satisfying shape, a way of relieving anxiety, of making life bearable. Sometimes this function of fiction is called a dirty and degrading word: "escapism." But it is not exactly that, any more than sleep is an escape from being awake, or a dream is an escape from not being in a dream, from being wherever we are when we are asleep and not dreaming. Sleep and dreaming are aspects of life which are important because they are necessary for our functioning as waking beings. A healthy person sleeps and dreams in order to awake refreshed. As sublimation, fiction takes our worst fears and tames them by organizing them in a form charged with meaning and value. Even the label "escapist" acknowledges that fiction is connected to our actual existence precisely by offering us relief from its problems and pressure. The flimsiest fairytale plays with our fears of death and failure by offering us a vicarious triumph over both of these terrors. And the tale of terror itself, like the nightmare, offers us finally the relief of escaping back from fiction into an actuality which seems sweet in mere contrast to the horrors of dream or fiction But the sublimation of anxiety and fear is only one of fiction's major functions. The other is cognition.

In its cognitive function, fiction helps us to know ourselves and our existential situation. Because fiction does function in this way, it has sometimes been assumed that it must offer us a record of experience or a picture of real life. This is the realistic fallacy, which so much of contemporary critical thought has labored to expose. For fiction offers us not transcriptions of actuality but systematic models which are distinct from reality, though they may be related to it in various ways. Traditionally, realists have claimed a close and direct correspondence between their models and the world around them This has led to disputes among them (like the well-known quarrels of Wells and James, or Bennett and Woolf) because each realist felt that his version of reality was called into question by someone else's different version. But to our eyes these disputes seem almost childish, since it is clear to us that these writers each presented in his work a model derived from a different aspect of reality and related to it in a different way. Every important writer's work offers us a different system of notation, which has its own focal limits in abstracting from the total system of existence.

The attempt of James Joyce in *Ulysses* to use a multiplicity of styles is a function of his awareness of the problem of notation. If each aspect of reality requires a different language, then Joyce would counter by generating an astonishing variety of narrative codes. But the very fact that Joyce persisted in the proliferation of codes in *Ulysses* indicates that he still subscribed to the realistic faith and was only resorting to extreme measures to preserve it. But now, with Joyce's example helping to clarify the nature of the problem, this faith is simply unavailable to those who consider carefully the possibilities of fiction. For what we can no longer accept is precisely this Joycean faith in the transcribability of things. It is because reality cannot be recorded that realism is dead. All writing, all composition, is construction. We do not imitate the world, we construct versions of it. There is no mimesis, only poiesis. No recording. Only constructing.

The failure of realism as a faith, however, is balanced by another failure which has been much less considered. And that is the failure of fantasy. For fantasy has claimed with considerable vigor a special status in literature. It has insisted that it is capable of non-realism, of an imaginative divorce between the fictional models it constructs and the world we all experience. This claim, too, has proved unfounded. No man has succeeded in imagining a world free of connection to our experiential world, with characters and situations that cannot be seen as mere inversions or distortions of that all too recognizable cosmos. Thus, if we must acknowledge that reality inevitably eludes our human languages, we must admit as well that these languages can never conduct the human imagination to a point beyond this reality. If we cannot reach it, neither can we escape it. And for the same reason: because we are in it. All fiction contributes to cognition, then, by providing us with models that reveal the nature of reality by their very failure to coincide with it. Though this distortion may be greater or lesser, there is always distortion. If there were not, there would be no cognition and no fiction; there would only be reality and us within it as the fish is in the sea and the sea is in the fish.

Some writers and critics have seen both sides of the fictional dilemma clearly. They know that reality can neither be captured nor escaped, and their response has been to redefine the esthetic act itself and argue that all works of the imagination are plagiaristic. The acceptance of this view by writers leads to the production of what has been called "self-reflective" fiction or "metafiction"—a fiction which, if it is "about" anything is about the possibilities and impossibilities of fiction itself, as in works like Barth's *Lost in the Funhouse* or Gass's *Willie Master's Lonesome Wife*. It also leads to the production of what might be called anticriticism—a criticism which denies the traditional critical imperatives without quite accepting the responsibilities of fiction. This anticriticism is widely practiced at present by such formidable figures as Susan Sontag and Ihab Hassan, as well as a host of lesser folk. It often involves a good deal of cutting and pasting, which is the critic's timid version of the writer's bold plagiarism.

What we have here is a classic case of loss of faith attended by abnegation of responsibilities. Everyone is expressing himself by copying everyone else, and, naturally, no one is listening. Nor is this situation to be dealt with by a few brisk exhortations. It is a philosophical problem and will require a philosophical answer. Which means that literary criticism should engage the problem itself and not merely wrestle with the symptoms of it. As Robert Coover pointed out in his metafictional *Pricksongs and Descants,* the contemporary writers of fiction "have been brought into a blind alley by critics and analysts." If there is a way out of this blind alley at present, it must be found by writers themselves, of course, but "critics and analysts" should at least feel obliged to help clarify the problem. And the problem is a complex one because it involves both those writers paralysed by solipsistic vertigo and those who have yet to experience it.

If self-reflective fiction is one response to this dilemma, what has been called the "new journalism" or the "non-fiction novel" is another. The best of the new journalists have accepted consciously or unconsciously the view I have been developing here, that both realism and fantasy are impossible achievements. Thus Norman Mailer and Tom Wolfe have adopted highly idiosyncratic or solipsistic attitudes in reacting to the people, situations, and events that they have dealt with in their writing. The reasoning behind much of the new journalism may be said to function in this way: "Since reality cannot be recorded, all pretense to objectivity is a sham therefore the only honest position is to admit one's subjectivity, even to flaunt it. And, on the other hand, since reality is

9

finally inescapable, there is bound to be some validity in my wildest flights of personal speculation. Ergo, whatever I feel like saying is worth hearing, and my method will be simply to let it all hang out." There is something to be said for the frankness and spontaniety of this position, but I think that it, too, is an overreaction to the loss of faith in realistic possibilities. Though all writing is construction, some models may well bear a useful and quite direct relationship to certain aspects of our human situation. It is precisely because the truth cannot be told that we must exercise such great skill and caution in trying to approach it.

Despite its weaknesses, the position of Wolfe and Mailer has more to recommend it than that of Truman Capote, for instance, who promises us boldly at the beginning of *In Cold Blood* that he will explain why the events he chronicles with such relish ever took place. The failure of this "why" to emerge from Capote's account is partly a measure of his bad faith and partly a failure of the realistic imagination. There is no single "why," of course, because there is no single omniscient perspective on human events. Capote has pretended to us that what is non-fictional will therefore be real or true—and this is simply not the case. The non-fiction novel pretends to offer both a record of the actual and the pleasure of novelistic certainty about the values involved in this record. Since it can deliver on neither of these promises, the attempt itself is fraudulent, and far less useful to us than the open solipsism of Wolfe and Mailer.

If both the metafictionists and the new journalists have failed to find viable, continuing solutions to the problem of linguistic limitations, they have done us a valuable service in exploring the nature of the problem, and they have produced individual works of strength and beauty—though how durable remains to be seen. Still, the problem remains. How can fiction be most useful to mankind in the present and the future? Can it function once again as a criticism of life with a validity beyond the merely personal? The solution, naturally, lies within the problem. If fictions are model versions of reality, rather than either records of the real or fabrications of the unreal, then we must explore the ways in which such models may relate to our existence. And here we may call upon the history of fiction to help us. For the relationship thought to exist between fictional models and reality has itself changed in time. If we, then, make a critical model intended to depict such change as a developing history, this model should enable us to make some projection into the future, and to speculate about the possible paths open to fiction at the present time. The model I wish to present here will take as its constructive focus an aspect of fictional history which is most apparent as an irreversible process changing through time. And that aspect is the treatment of fictional time itself.

Every fictional work presents a model which stands in some temporal relation to the world of its composition. This seems simple enough, but it is complicated by the fact that time itself has been

11

conceived of differently at different points of history. Mythic fictions are produced in cultures that lack a concept of historical time. Myths deal with unchanging conditions. If they treat the creation of the world—as they often do—they present it as establishing conditions of existence which will remain fixed until the end of time. When myths deal with the time between the Beginning and the End, they treat this time as cyclical not as linear. This view of the cosmos persists in primitive cultures until certain technical developments (such as the invention of writing) force them to acknowledge that history exists and they are in it.

Closely related to mythic time is legendary time. Fictions of legendary time represent a stage in the growth of historical awareness. Legendary time has two stages, a "then" and a "now." Then, there were giants in the earth, or a paradise inhabited by man. Now, men are smaller and the conditions of existence are more constricting. Sometimes legendary time includes the notion of a future (a "then" in the other direction) in which lost greatness will be restored and paradise regained. Legendary time thus incorporates some notions of past, present, and future, but as distinct conditions—as beginning, middle, and end, rather than as a continuous process of change functioning through specific human actions. Legendary time should be distinguished from another concept which is also rooted in primitive culture though never entirely supplanted, even in the most technologically developed societies. This is the ideal time of fairy tale and romance, a time out of time, which offers us neither beginning, middle, nor end of our own historical process but another time altogether, a time "upon a time"—a whole parallel universe where events are ordered nearer our hearts' desires than they are in this world.

As cultures enter history all three of these narrative time-concepts are altered. Myth atrophies, becomes fixed, an artifact from a vanished world. Ideal time retreats to the less sophisticated enclaves in a given culture: the folk, the children, the disabled and disadvantaged. Or it persists as something condescendingly tolerated by the cultural initiates as an "opiate for the masses." But it does not die, nor does the need of all men to live in ideal time at regular intervals vanish. Daydreams and nightdreams are inevitable, and even the worst nightmares have the inevitable happy ending of the sleeper's discovering that "it was only a dream." When we wake into the nightmare of history, however, this is another story. The third form of primitive time-consciousness that we are considering here—legendary time—slowly evolves into historical time. In the very writing of history we can see this process. Herodotus leads to Thucydides, Livy gives way to Tacitus, and even Gibbon seems but a teller of tales along side of Rostovtzeff.

As the shift is made in human consciousness from legendary time to historical time, many other changes also occur. When history is discerned as a

13

continuous process, the past and the present are perceived as intimately related. At first recurrent cycles are noted, in which history seems to repeat itself. But finally the irreversibility of certain historical processes becomes clear. At this point man may be said to be fully aware that he is *in* history, as a raft is in a river, and that some things, once passed, will never be seen again. The writing of fiction has of course been deeply influenced by these developments. The novel itself may be said to have developed and reached its greatest achievements precisely by learning to regard the present as history. The rise of the novel as a narrative form was marked by a shift from concern with a legendary past to concern with a historical present. By the nineteenth century the novel had clearly established as its *raison d'être* the recording of changes in human behavior. This is precisely what the great realists, from Balzac to Zola, thought they were accomplishing. But something else happened in the nineteenth century, which changed the possibilities for fiction in ways that are just beginning to be realized.

The consciousness that history is an irreversible process led man inevitably to a new view of the future. For centuries man had thought of the future as in one sense inscrutable, except as darkly hinted at by oracles and portents, and in another sense as simply more of the present. One might not know who would be king but one knew that there would always be one. The King is dead? Long live the King! The idea that the future might be radically different in its social or economic organization was unthinkable until some time in the seventeenth or eighteenth century, and the impact of irreversible technological change did not become apparent until the nineteenth. The result of these and other developments was that man could finally conceive of the future historically. Having reclaimed the past from legend and the present from chronicle, writers of realistic fiction could begin contemplating the future as a space of time about which novels might be written. But something happens to realism when it is projected into the future. (Something happens to realism projected backward into the past, too, but that is not our concern here.) The idea of a future different from the present, but logically connected to it by developments of present circumstances, gradually impressed itself on writers during the latter part of the nineteenth century. Then utopian fictions, which had always been located outside of human time, could be projected into a historical future and linked to the present by imaginative extrapolation. And such works began to appear, as did projections of a disastrous, dystopian future. The first ventures of novelists into the historical future were mainly of the utopian/dystopian kind, or else were technological romances like those of Jules Verne, in which boyish men played with new toys created by science. But over the past century the possibilities of future-fiction have been greatly extended. And,

15

what is more important, the rate of change in the present human situation has accelerated dramatically. At the same time, and this is the most important change of all, humanity has acquired and is acquiring an unprecedented power to affect its own future.

Recently, as I completed a book on structuralism in literature, I found myself writing the following words on the final page:

> Man exists in a system beyond his control but not beyond his power to rearrange. The fall of man is neither a myth from pre-history nor an event at the beginning of human time. It is a process that has been occuring for centuries, and it is not so much a fall into knowledge as into power—the power to work great changes in ourselves and our immediate environment, the power to destroy our planet in various ways, slowly or quickly, or to maintain it and our life upon it for some time. On various levels of activity, man's ability to exert his power in self-destructive ways exceeds the ability of his feedback systems to correct his behavior. The great failures of our government in recent years have been failures of imagination. What we need in all areas of life is more sensitive and vigorous feed-back. The role of a properly structuralist imagination will of necessity be futuristic. It will inform mankind of the consequences of actions not yet taken. But it must not merely inform, it must make us feel the consequences of those action, feel them in our hearts and our viscera. The structuralist imagination must help us to live in the future so that we can indeed continue to live in the future. And this task, this great task, as it makes itself felt, will work its changes in the

system of literature. New forms will arise, must arise, if man is to continue.

Now, contemplating the situation of contemporary fiction specifically, I find myself drawn to the same conclusion. The future, in the immortal words of Mort Sahl, "lies ahead." The future of fiction lies in the future.

This apparently tautological statement will bear some examination. I am asserting that the most appropriate kind of fiction that can be written in the present and the immediate future is fiction that takes place in future time. And this assertion is based on several lines of argument which I have been presenting here. First, there is the historical argument. My model of fictional history suggests that this move into future-fiction is itself an appropriate historical development, for this form of fiction has been gathering strength for about a century and is currently coming into dominance. Second, there is the ethical argument, which I have only touched on briefly. According to this argument, our need for future feedback to guide present action makes writers of fiction responsible for the production of imaginative models of the future, alternative projections that can give us some sense of the consequences of present actions. If we accept Jean-Paul Sartre's imperative for literature, that it be a force for improvement of the human situation, and if we nevertheless would not see fiction reduced to the level of propaganda, then

17

the idea of fiction freely speculating on possible futures must appeal to us.

The third line of argument behind my plea for a future-fiction is a metaphysical one, for it involves the resolution of the solipsistic problem that has proved so crucial for modern fiction. Projected into the future, the problems of realism and fantasy both vanish. There is no question of "recording" the future, nor of denying its actualities. All future projection is obviously model-making, poiesis not mimesis. And freed of the problem of correspondence or noncorrespondence with some present actuality or some previously experienced past, with its records and recollections, the imagination can function without self-deception as to its means and ends. Projections can be held tightly to a line of greatest probability, extrapolating from perceptions of current reality according to current notions of what is probable. But it is also possible to project more freely, discarding as many current notions as possible, or accepting as likely things that now seem unlikely. Because we know that the unexpected happens continually in the history of science itself, fiction has now a license to speculate as freely as it may, in the hope of offering us glimmers of a reality hidden from us by our present set of preconceptions. In the future, realism and fantasy must have a more intricate and elaborate relationship with one another. The models made by scientists frequently prove to have predictive power. That is, in fact, the common way of establishing their validity. The models of future-fiction need not operate in quite the same way, but they will frequently have a power of their own, which was described by one of the great neglected authors of modern British fiction, Olaf Stapledon. Back in 1930, in the preface to his seminal work of fictional projection, *Last and First Men,* Stapledon described his kind of writing in the following way:

> To romance of the future may seem to be indulgence in ungoverned speculation for the sake of the marvellous. Yet controlled imagination in this sphere can be a very valuable exercise for minds bewildered about the present and its potentialities. Today we should welcome, and even study, every serious attempt to envisage the future of our race; not merely in order to grasp the very diverse and often tragic possibilities that confront us, but also that we may familiarize ourselves with the certainty that many of our most cherished ideals would seem puerile to more developed minds. To romance of the far future, then, is to attempt to see the human race in its cosmic setting, and to mould our hearts to entertain new values.
>
> But if such imaginative construction of possible futures is to be at all potent, our imagination must be strictly disciplined. We must endeavor not to go beyond the bounds of possibility set by the particular state of culture within which we live. The merely fantastic has only minor power. Not that we should seek actually to prophesy what will as a matter of fact occur; for in our present state such prophecy is certainly futile, save in the simplest matters. We are not set up as historians

attempting to look ahead instead of backwards. We can only select a certain thread out of the tangle of many equally valid possibilities. But we must select with a purpose. The activity that we are undertaking is not science, but art; and the effect that it should have on the reader is the effect that art should have.

Yet our aim is not merely to create aesthetically admirable fiction. We must achieve neither mere history, nor mere fiction, but myth. A true myth is one which, within the universe of a certain culture (living or dead), expresses richly, and often perhaps tragically, the highest admirations possible within that culture. A false myth is one which either violently transgresses the limits of credibility set by its own cultural matrix, or expresses admirations less developed than those of its culture's best vision.[1]

Stapledon used the word "myth" rather differently from the way I have employed that term here (in my more limited sense of the word, myth can no longer be produced), but his meaning is plain. He sees future-fiction as a way of subjecting current values to a "higher" set of values obtained by extrapolating from man's present "admirations." This is one formulation, among many that could be made, of the serious value of "romances of the future." And Stapledon himself, in works like *Last and First Men* and *The Star Maker*, has given ample evidence of the unique power of his personal vision. (Here we may note that Penguin Books' recent issuing of his major works from the thirties

[1] *Last and First Men* (Baltimore: Penguin Books, 1972), pp. 11-12.

and forties is a sign pointing to the coming rehabilitation of Stapledon as an important figure in the literary history of this century.)

My fourth line of argument on behalf of future-fiction is based on my model of the current fictional scene itself. I have already sketched the dilemma of self-reflective fiction and the new journalism, and will not repeat that here, but move on to examine the situations of traditional realistic fiction and of what is called science fiction. There is a traditional fiction being published today that is immensely successful in the marketplace though it has no critical approbation and probably deserves little. This fiction is truly "popular" in that it stays carefully within established generic lines and established formulae of expression. Most of our fictional best-sellers—Jacqueline Susann, Leon Uris, the *Airports* and *Hospitals* of our literary world—fall into this category. It features a strong narrative line, characters with whom readers identify, and a comforting "realism" that purports to explain how things really work in contemporary society, even to the point of suggesting that many of the fictional personages presented are actually real people whose names we all know—especially those people whose "private lives" are followed so publicly in the *National Enquirer* and similar scandal sheets. This sort of fiction has one important thing—readers. But it pays a high price for its readership, and they pay a high price for their pleasure, for they are led to believe in a "reality" which is

21

irrelevant to our actual situation in many respects. And precisely because they believe in this reality, they are dangerously uninformed as citizens and human beings who must face real problems.

There is also, of course, a more serious traditional fiction which still operates on largely realistic principles. It, too, has its successes, which may be represented here by Saul Bellow in America and C. P. Snow in England, who have both been commercially successful and critically esteemed—though perhaps not equally. This tradition (in my model of the present situation) is in trouble of various sorts, lacking both young readers and strong young writers—but the problem of readership is the most acute. Serious treatment of contemporary life in the realistic manner is having trouble maintaining its audience. My perception of this problem is similar to that of Charles Newman, who discussed the subject eloquently in *TriQuarterly* No. 26. But where Newman laid the problem at the door of the distribution system—"a handmade art in a mass production economy"—I see the problem as an aspect of our lost faith in the language of realism, which includes both our suspicion of present omniscience and our need for some clear sense of the future. A great part of this attitude is simple impatience with chronicles of the present, impatience with psychological self-scrutiny, impatience with the details of a time that seems long gone before it can be reduced to words, edited, printed, and distributed. But, impatience aside, we will turn to the new journalists if it is chronicle we want. From fiction we expect a more conscious model-building, a more deliberate imaginative process.

This same impatience with fictional chronicling becomes more evident each year in one place where it cannot be ignored—in the work produced by contemporary realistic writers. It is not only the Barths, Pynchons, Goldings, and Durrells who are producing novels that approach the methods and concerns of science fiction, but writers who have considerable experience with and commitment to chronicling, like Anthony Burgess, whose Malayan chronicle has been followed by some brilliant excursions into the future—not only the ubiquitous *Clockwork Orange,* but the less well-known and richer *Wanting Seed* as well. One could cite Walker Percy's *Love in the Ruins* as a similar example of a writer whose concern for the present has led him to romance of the future, and there are other parallel cases, but the most instructive that I know of is the case of Doris Lessing.

For years Doris Lessing has been a classic example of the autobiographical realist who must wait between each book in order to live through enough material to fuel the next one. What, then, is one to make of the conclusion of her five-volume chronicle of the life of Martha Quest, *Children of Violence,* which in the last pages of the last volume calmly moves into the future, after the atomic catastrophe, and accepts as realities various kinds of

23

extrasensory perception which are forbidden to realism by our current standards of scientific probability? What indeed? My reading of Ms. Lessing's move into the future is a simple one. She has moved with the times and sees that the future is the only lever with which we can hope to nudge the present in a better direction—which is what Stapledon saw, what Orwell saw, what Wells saw, what Huxley saw, and what the best contemporary writers of science fiction also see. Robert Coover once wrote that we must use "the fabulous to probe beyond the phenomenological, beyond appearances, beyond randomly perceived events, beyond mere history."[2] What Doris Lessing has discovered, and I honor her for it, is that we must use the future in precisely the same way, as a probe into the truth of the present.

Now, in making these arguments I may have suggested too strongly that the value of science fiction depends on its practical didatic quality— that it is good because it will make life better. If so, I must try to redress that balance a bit. Fiction alone will neither make us better nor improve the quality of our world. It can help us to see the consequences of present action; it can help solidify for us the reality of our theoretical values; but it can only change our minds if the world itself provides confirmation of its fictional modeling. A

[2] Robert Coover, *Pricksongs and Descants* (New York: E. P. Dutton, 1969), p. 78.

24

major didactic function of future-fiction may simply be, as Michael Ryan has suggested, to help us loosen our grip upon the present and accept the future as real. Our heritage from the past century, from its dominant forms of fiction and its dominant styles of life, has been intensely materialistic and "propertarian." We must grow away from these values. We must learn to relinquish our tight grip on the present moment and its immediate pleasure, in order to live in harmony with a cosmos that won't stand still, in which there are no epiphanies, no revelations, only transformations. The total mental effect of reading extensively in the fiction of the future may be to relieve us of anxiety about the present—a relief which can only make that present itself more easily and happily endured. But what I have been calling future-fiction is not entirely about—nor simply about—the future of man. We need to view this fiction in a wider perspective than the temporal one—which will be the aim of the following lecture.

2

The Roots of Science Fiction

ALL FICTION—EVERY BOOK EVEN, FICTION OR NOT
—takes us out of the world we normally inhabit. To
enter a book is to live in another place. Out of the
nature of this otherness and its relation to our life
experiences come all our theories of interpretation
and all our criteria of value. In the previous lecture
I argued the case for a particular relation between
fiction and experience, expressed in temporal
terms as "future-fiction." The polemical nature of
my situation as advocate for a popular but critically deprecated form of fiction led me inevitably
to make a case which is in certain respects too
narrow for its subject. The laws of rhetoric force
all radical advocates to choose between betraying
their causes by an excess of conciliation or of
hostility, and I understand those laws only too
well. In compensation, I wish to be more tentative
and speculative now, in describing the parameters
of a fictional form that is both old and new, rooted
in the past but distinctly modern, oriented to the
future but not bounded by it.

It is customary in our empirically based Anglo-Saxon criticism to distinguish between two great schools of fiction according to the relationship between the fictional worlds they present and the world of human experience. Thus we have, since the eighteenth century, spoken of novels and romances, of realism and fantasy, and we have found the distinction useful enough at times, even though, because of our empirical bias, we have tended to value realism more highly than romance. It will be appropriate, then, at least as a beginning, to see the tradition that leads to modern science fiction as a special case of romance, for this tradition always insists upon a radical discontinuity between its world and the world of ordinary human experience. In its simplest and most ancient form this discontinuity is objectified as another world, a different place: Heaven, Hell, Eden, Fairyland, Utopia, The Moon, Atlantis, Lilliput. This radical dislocation between the world of romance and the world of experience has been exploited in different ways. One way, the most obvious, has been to suspend the laws of nature in order to give more power to the laws of narrative, which are themselves projections of the human psyche in the form of enacted wishes and fears. These pure enactments are at the root of all narrative structures, are themselves the defining characteristics of all narrative forms, whether found in "realistic" or "fantastic" matrices. In the sublimative narratives of pure romance they are merely more obvious than elsewhere because less disguised by other interests and qualities. But there is another way to exploit the radical discontinuity between the world of romance and that of experience, and this way emphasizes cognition. The difference can be used to get a more vigorous purchase on certain aspects of that very reality which has been set aside in order to generate a romantic cosmos. When romance returns deliberately to confront reality it produces the various forms of didactic romance or fabulation that we usually call allegory, satire, fable, parable, and so on—to indicate our recognition that reality is being addressed indirectly through a patently fictional device.

Fabulation, then, is fiction that offers us a world clearly and radically discontinuous from the one we know, yet returns to confront that known world in some cognitive way. Traditionally, it has been a favorite vehicle for religious thinkers, precisely because religions have insisted that there is more to the world than meets the eye, that the common-sense view of reality—"realism"—is incomplete and therefore false. Science, of course, has been telling us much the same thing for several hundred years. The world we see and hear and feel—"reality" itself—is a fiction of our senses, and dependent on their focal ability, as the simplest microscope will easily demonstrate. Thus it is not surprising that what we call "science" fiction should employ the same narrative vehicle as the religious fictions of our past. In a sense, they are

29

fellow travellers. But there are also great differences between these kinds of fiction, which must be investigated.

There are two varieties of fabulation or didactic romance, which corresponds roughly to the distinction between romances of religion and romances of science. We may call these two forms "dogmatic" and "speculative" fabulation, respectively. This distinction is neither complete nor invidious. It represents a tendency rather than delineating a type, but most didactic romances are clearly dominated by one tendency or the other. Even within the Christian tradition, we can recognize Dante's *Commedia* as a dogmatic fabulation and More's *Utopia* as a speculative one. Dante's work is greater by most accepted standards of comparison. But it works out of a closed, anti-speculative system of belief. A *Utopia* admits in its title that it is nowhere. A *Commedia,* human or divine, on the other hand, must fill the known cosmos. As opposed to dogmatic narrative, speculative fabulation is a creature of humanism, associated from its origins with attitudes and values that have shaped the growth of science itself. Swift detested the science of his time, which drove him to dogmatic posturing in Book III of *Gulliver.* But surely without the microscope and telescope Books I and II could not have been as they are. And Book IV is a speculation beyond all dogma. Since Dante, dogmatic fabulation has declined, though it always lurks in the worlds of satire. Since More, speculative fabulation has grown and developed. Born of humanism it has been fostered by science. But it has never flourished as it does at present—for reasons that it is now our business to explore.

As Claudio Guillén has taught us, literature may be usefully seen as aspiring toward system—as a collection of entities constantly rearranging themselves in search of an equilibrium never achieved. In the course of this process certain generic forms crystallize and persist or fade from existence, and among these forms some come into dominance at particular moments of history, only to yield their dominant position with the passage of time. In every age, as the Russian Formalists were fond of observing, certain generic forms are regarded as "canonical"—the accepted forms for the production of serious literature—and other forms are considered outside the pale, being either too esoteric ("coterie literature") or too humble ("popular literature"). But with the passage of time canonical forms become rigid, heavy, mannered, and lose their vital power. Even the dominant forms eventually give up their privileged position and move toward the edges of the literary canon. The reasons for this may be seen in purely formal terms—as the exhaustion of the expressive resources of the genre. Or they may be seen in broader cultural terms—as responses to social or conceptual developments outside the literary system itself. To my way of thinking, since fiction is a cognitive art it cannot be considered adequately in purely formal terms. Formal changes, to be understood, must be seen in the light of other changes in the human situation.

I propose, then, to examine a small but important part of the system of literature: the interaction of certain forms of fictional representation over a period of a few centuries, ending with the present time. And I further propose to see this interaction as an aspect of a larger movement of mind. My treatment will be extremely brief; the model I generate will be very sketchy. But in matters of this kind true persuasion is not to be achieved by the amassing of argumentative detail. I ask you simply to consider the fictional universe from the perspective of this model and then see if your old perspective can ever be comfortably assumed again. I will begin by raising a question seldom considered—perhaps because it is too large to admit of an answer. The question is, simply, "What makes a form dominant?" Admitting the phenomenon of dominance, why, for instance, should drama dominate the western countries of Europe for a hundred years from the late sixteenth through the seventeenth century? In general terms it has been argued, and I think convincingly, that drama was ideally suited to an era in which monolithic feudalism had lost its power over individual existence but bourgeois democracy had not yet come into being as a regulator of the power vacuum left behind by the crumbling feudal system. An age of princes (in the Machiavellian sense) made heroic drama conceivable as neither an earlier age of kings nor a later age of ministers ever could. The dramatic disposition of the age, with its incredible reversals of fortune, as seen, for instance, in the life of an Essex or a Ralegh, enabled a specific literary form to realize its maximum potential.

In the case of the novel, we find a form that came into dominance for parallel cultural reasons. The rise of the middle class did not "cause" the rise of the novel, but new concepts of the human situation enabled both of these phenomena to take place. In particular, a new grasp of history, as a process with its own dynamics resulting from the interaction of social and economic forces, generated a new concept of man as a creature struggling against these impersonal entitites. And this struggle could hardly be represented on the stage in the same way as man's struggle with fortune or his own ambitious desires. It is not that plays dealing with socio-economic man could not be written. Writers from Steele to Ibsen struggled manfully to generate a rich social canvas on stage. But what the novel achieved easily and naturally, the drama could do only with great pains and clumsy inadequacy. The novel naturally came to be the literary form in which an age conscious of history as a shaping force could express itself most satisfyingly. The novel was the diachronic form of a diachronic age. In each volume of the great nineteenth-century realists we find the history of an individual against a background of the forces shaping his moment of history. And in the sequences of novels produced by writers like Balzac and Zola we can see whole eras taking human shape, becoming protagonists struggling in the grip of the large designs of History itself. For this, of course, was the age in which History acquired a capital H, becoming a substitute for God, with a Grand Purpose in Mind, which His angel the Time-Spirit sought to effect.

Let us narrow the focus, now, to the narrative forms of representation only, for dominance can be considered not only among the great generic kinds, and even among whole arts, but also within the boundaries of a single kind of literature. In the novel itself we can trace the rise and fall from dominance of sentimental fiction in the eighteenth century, of a more sociological and historical fiction in the nineteenth, and finally a more inward and psychological fiction in the early twentieth century. All of these forms have gone under the name of realism, and as an evolving tradition this realism preserved a dominant place among the forms of fiction from the time of Defoe and Marivaux until well into the present century. Other fictional forms have coexisted with the dominant realism—such as the gothic, which first emerged in the late eighteenth century to fill an emotive gap opened in the system by the move of social and sentimental forms away from situations of heroic intensity. And after Swift a speculative fabulation with satirical tendencies was kept alive by writers like Johnson in *Rasselas* and Carlyle in *Sartor Re-*

sartus. But it is fair to say that this tradition lacked vigor and continuity—lacked generic certainty— until new conceptual developments put fictional speculation on an entirely different footing, changing the fabric of man's vision in ways that inevitably led to changes in his fiction.

This revolution in man's conception of himself was begun by Darwin's theory of evolution. It was continued by Einstein's theory of relativity. And it has been extended by developments in the study of human systems of perception, organization, and communication that range from the linguistic philosophy of Wittgenstein and the gestalt psychology of Köhler to the structural anthropology of Lévi-Strauss and the cybernetics of Wiener. This century of cosmic rearrangement, crudely indicated here by this list of names and concepts, has led to new ways of understanding human time and space-time, as well as to a new sense of the relationship between human systems and the larger systems of the cosmos. In its broadest sense, this revolution, has replaced Historical Man with Structural Man.

Let us explore this great mental shift a bit. Darwin, and those who have continued his work, put human history in a frame of reference much grander than that of Historical Man. This stretched man's entire sense of time into a new shape and finally altered his familiar position in the cosmos. Early reactions to the evolutionary theory often tried to accommodate Darwinian evolutionary theory within the familiar dimensions of historical time, suggesting that some Superman lurked just around the evolutionary corner—in much the same way that people once believed the apocalypse to be scheduled for the very near future. But by expanding our sense of time the Darwinians reduced history to a moment and man to a bit player in a great unfinished narrative. The possibility of further evolution, with species more advanced than ourselves coming into being on this earth, displaced man from the final point of traditional cosmic teleology as effectively as Galileo had displaced man's planet from the center of the spatial cosmos. Thus Darwinian time, which has been continually extended with the discovery of new geological and archeological evidence, has had a profound effect on man's sense of himself and his possibilities. Historical time, then, is only a tiny fragment of human time, which is again a tiny fragment of geologic time, which is itself only a bit of cosmic time.

The theories of relativity have worked in a similar fashion to shake man out of his humanist perspective. By demonstrating that space and time are in a more intimate perspectival relation than we had known, Einstein too called history into question. When we think in terms of the cosmic distances and absolute velocities of the Einsteinian universe, not only do we lose our grasp on fundamental human concepts like "simultaneity" and "identity," we lose also our confidence in that common-sense apprehension of the world which replaced man's mythic consciousness as the novel replaced the epic in the hierarchy of narrative forms. And on the smaller scale of purely human studies in anthropology, psychology, and linguistics, ideas no less earthshaking have been developed. What does it do to our time sense to think of stone-age men living their timeless lives in the year 1974 in some remote jungle on our earth? And what does it do to our confidence in human progress when we see that though they lack all the things that our science and technology have given us, they live in a harmony with the cosmos that shames us, and know instinctively, it seems, lessons that we are painfully relearning by having to face the consequences of our ecological wantonness? At every turn we run into patterns of shaping force that have gone unobserved by our instrumental approach to the world. We learn that men's visual perceptions are governed by mental leaps to whole configurations or "gestalts" rather than by patient accumulation of phenomenal details. We learn that we acquire language in similar quantum jumps of grammatical competence. And we know that our acquired languages in turn govern and shape our perceptions of this world. Finally, we have begun to perceive that our social systems and our linguistic systems share certain similarities of pattern, that even our most intimate forms of behavior are ordered by behavioral configurations beyond our perception and controlled through biological feedback systems that may be altered by the input of various drugs, hormones, and other biochemical messages.

In short, we are now so aware of the way that our lives are part of a patterned universe that we are free to speculate as never before. Where anything may be true—sometime, someplace—there can be no heresy. And where the patterns of the cosmos itself guide our thoughts so powerfully, so beautifully, we have nothing to fear but our own lack of courage. There are fields of force around us that even our finest instruments of thought and perception are only beginning to detect. The job of fiction is to play in these fields. And in the past few decades fiction has begun to do just this, to dream new dreams, confident that there is no gate of ivory, only a gate of horn, and that all dreams are true.   It is fiction—verbal narrative—that must take the lead in such dreaming, because even the new representational media that have been spawned in this age cannot begin to match the speculative agility and imaginative freedom of words. The camera can capture only what is found in front of it or made for it, but language is as swift as thought itself and can reach beyond what is, or seems, to what may or may not be, with the speed of a synapse. Until the mind can speak in its own tongueless images, the word will be its fleetest and most delicate instrument of communication. It is not strange, then, that the modern revolution in human thought should find expression in a transformation of a form of fictional speculation that has been available for centuries. It took only a quantum jump in fictional evolution for speculative fabulation to become structural, and the mutation took place sometime early in this century.

What, then, is structural fabulation? I shall begin to explore specific instances of this modern fictional form in my next lecture, but here it will be appropriate to sketch the parameters of the form in a general way, as a preparation for that discussion. Considered generically, structural fabulation is simply a new mutation in the tradition of speculative fiction. It is the tradition of More, Bacon, and Swift, as modified by new input from the physical and human sciences. Considered as an aspect of the whole system of contemporary fiction, it has grown in proportion to the decline of other fictional forms. For instance, to the extent that the dominant realistic novel has abandoned the pleasures of narrative movement for the cares of psychological and social analysis, a gap in the system has developed which a number of lesser forms have sought to fill. All the forms of adventure fiction, from western, to detective, to spy, to costume— have come into being in response to the movement of "serious" fiction away from plot and the pleasures of fictional sublimation. Because many human beings experience a psychological need for narration—whether cultural or biological in origin— the literary system *must* include works which answer to that need. But when the dominant canonical form fails to satisfy such a basic drive, the system becomes unbalanced. The result is that readers resort secretly and guiltily to lesser forms for that narrative fix they cannot do without. And many feel nearly as guilty about it as we could hope to make any habitual offender against our official mores. The spectacle (reported by George Moore, as I recollect) of W. B. Yeats explaining with great embarrassment why he happened to be reading a detective story can stand as a paradigm of the guilt felt by intellectuals whose emotional needs drive them to lesser literary forms for pleasure. We do call people "addicts" if they seem inordinately fond of detective stories, or even of science fiction. But the metaphor of addiction is a dangerously misleading one. For this is emotional food, not a mind-bending narcotic, that we are considering.

Thus the vacuum left by the movement of "serious" fiction away from storytelling has been filled by "popular" forms with few pretentions to any virtues beyond those of narrative excitement. But the very emptiness of these forms, as they are usually managed, has left another gap, for forms which supply readers' needs for narration without starving their needs for intellection. The "letdown" experienced after finishing many detective stories or adventure tales comes from a sense of time wasted—time in which we have deliberately suspended not merely our sense of disbelief but also far too many of our normal cognitive processes. And this letdown grows to a genuine and appropriate feeling of guilt to the extent that we *do* become addicted and indulge in the reading of such stories beyond our normal need for diversion and sublimation. Even food should not be taken in abnormal quantities, especially if much of it is empty calories. We require a fiction which satisfies our cognitive and sublimative needs together, just as we want food which tastes good and provides some nourishment. We need suspense with intellectual consequences, in which questions are raised as well as solved, and in which our minds are expanded even while focused on the complications of a fictional plot.

These may be described as our general requirements—needs which have existed as long as man has been sufficiently civilized to respond to a form that combines sublimation and cognition. But we also have to consider here the special requirements of our own age—our need for fictions which provide a sublimation relevant to the specific conditions of being in which we find ourselves. The most satisfying fictional response to these needs takes the form of what may be called structural fabulation. In works of structural fabulation the tradition of speculative fiction is modified by an awareness of the nature of the universe as a system of systems, a structure of a structures, and the insights of the past century of science are accepted as fictional points of departure. Yet structural fabulation is neither scientific in its methods nor a substitute for actual science. It is a fictional exploration of hu-

41

man situations made perceptible by the implications of recent science. Its favorite themes involve the impact of developments or revelations derived from the human or the physical sciences upon the people who must live with those revelations or developments.

In the previous era, historicist views of human culture led to a vision of man's future as guided by some plan beyond human comprehension, perhaps, in its totality, but solicitous of man and amenable to human cooperation. Thus great fictional narratives could be couched in terms of individual men and women seeking to align themselves with or struggle against the social forces through which History was working its Will to achieve its Idea. But now structuralism dominates our thought, with its view of human existence as a random happening in a world which is orderly in its laws but without plan or purpose. Thus man must learn to live within laws that have given him his being but offer him no purpose and promise him no triumph as a species. Man must make his own values, fitting his hopes and fears to a universe which has allowed him a place in its systematic working, but which cares only for the system itself and not for him. Man must create his future himself. History will not do it for him. And the steps he has already taken to modify the biosphere can be seen as limiting the future options of the human race. It is in this atmosphere that structural fabulation draws its breath, responding to these conditions of being, in the form of extrapolative narrative. The extrapolations may be bold and philosophical or cautious and sociological, but they must depart from what we know and consider what we have due cause to hope and fear. Like all speculative fabulations they will take their origin in some projected dislocation of our known existence, but their projections will be based on a contemporary apprehension of the biosphere as an ecosystem and the universe as a cosmosystem.

Obviously, not all works that are called "science fiction" meet this kind of standard. Many writers are so deficient in their understanding of the cosmic structure itself that they have no sense of the difference between purposeful discontinuity and a magical relaxation of the cosmic structure. And many others seek to present traditional romance as if it had some structural or speculative significance. But, if a writer fails to understand the discontinuity on which his work is based *as* a discontinuity *from* a contemporary view of what is true or natural, he is powerless to make that discontinuity function structurally for us. Thus any cognitive thrust in his work will be accidental and intermittent. And if a writer transports men to Mars merely to tell a cowboy story, he produces not structural fabulation but star dreck—harmless, perhaps, but an abuse of that economy of means that governs mature esthetic satisfaction. Or if he allows such a variety of magical events that his fictional world seems deficient in its own natural laws, his work will fail structurally and cognitively, too, though it may retain some sublimative force. But in the most admirable of structural fabulations, a radical discontinuity between the fictional world and our own provides both the means of narrative suspense and of speculation. In the perfect structural fabulation, idea and story are so wedded as to afford us simultaneously the greatest pleasures that fiction provides: sublimation and cognition.

3

Structural Fabulation

I BEGAN THESE LECTURES BY REMARKING THAT knowing one thing is a way of not knowing something else. And I will add now that this situation is the major problem in all communicative experiences—of which art is one and education is another. When we attempt to communicate, we send a message to another person. That person receives the set of signs that constitutes our message—and he interprets it. Reading our message in the light of his own verbal experience, his own values, his own premises, this person, this reader, inevitably shapes our message, bends it in the direction of his heart's desire. And this we call understanding. In teaching poetry, for instance, the instructor's great problem is to prevent students from laying on a poem whatever convenient, comfortable meaning they have readily available—instead of attending to the meanings of the poem itself. What is most required in the reading of poetry is a suspension not of disbelief but of belief

45

itself—a suspension of interpretation as long as possible, so that it may be, when it comes, richly responsive to the particular verbal configurations of this utterance. We leap to familiar meanings as we leap to recognize the person of someone we know from a glimpse of a face or the shadow of a gesture. All our interpretive processes proceed in quantum jumps from apprehended parts to imagined wholes or gestalts.

The problem of the writer, then, is to prevent our making this leap to the familiar. As Victor Shklovksy and Samuel Coleridge knew, the writer must upset our habitual perceptions in order to make us see the world freshly. Art exists, in Shklovksy's beautiful phrase, to make the stone stony. Professor Darko Suvin, in the best essay on science fiction that I have seen ("On the Poetics of the Science Fiction Genre," *College English,* Dec. 1972, pp. 372-382), argues that the fundamental principle of science fiction is precisely this technique of defamiliarization or estrangement. But this has been the premise of all art since the romantic period. It is not unique to SF. What is unique in this form of fiction is the way in which it defamiliarizes things. In the worlds of SF we are made to see the stoniness of a stone by watching it move and change in an accelerated time-scale, or by encountering an anti-stone with properties so unstony that we are forced to reinvestigate the true quality of stoniness. In Shklovsky's theory it is the *form* of the message which restores stoniness to the

46

stone. Because the message is complex, difficult—in a word, poetical—it prevents our habitual response and opens our eyes to the reality of the object. But in SF this estrangement is more conceptual and less verbal. It is the new idea that shocks us into perception, rather than the new language of the poetic text. And it is precisely because of this that our old formalistic methodology seldom works well as a critical approach to SF. This approach itself has functioned as a great block to our perception of the richness and beauty of a new fictional mutation. The analytical tools fashioned to deal with Flaubert and James will not work so well with writers operating from a quite different set of premises.

The problem of "knowing" as a block to understanding is especially acute, then, in the critical reception of science fiction. Rarely has a genre existed about which so many people have firm opinions without any direct experience of its major texts. And what are some of the things which the traditional literary critic knows about SF? He knows that works of SF use the language clumsily, with neither grace nor wit. He knows that these works lack interesting characters, being populated by robots, some of whom are supposed to be men and women. He knows that the plotting in these fictions is either hackneyed, episodic, or both. And he knows that their subject matter is unreal, escapist, and ultimately trivial.

This is a heavy weight of knowledge, indeed, and

47

I am not sure how far these four lectures can go to remove it and open the way for understanding. Moreover, the removal itself is complicated by the fact that there is some truth in this set of prejudices. For instance, SF *is* less concerned with individual psychology than some earlier forms of fiction have been. But I would point out that this is also true of other contemporary kinds of fabulation—and some ancient fictional classics as well. Furthermore, this de-emphasis of psychological individuality is definitely not a way of abandoning human emotions and concerns. I have been moved deeply by many works of structural fabulation, and moved to think seriously about the human situation. Characters may be realized in many ways other than those of psychological analysis. Yet it is fair to say that the representation of unique individuality is not so much an end in itself in SF as it has been in some realistic novels. Plot is much more likely to be an end in itself for the SF writer, and when this happens we get space opera rather than structural fabulation. But here, as in other forms, there is an immense difference between the careful and systematically plotted work and the careless, forgetful one. And as plot becomes systematized, it approaches the structural and cognitive.

The question of language in SF is perhaps more crucial. And here again it is fair to say that much SF is written in journeyman's prose, serviceable but inelegant. Can important ideas be conveyed in such prose? It is an interesting question. Some ideas are so refined that without a refined language they could not exist. Others are less refined, but not necessarily less powerful. Sometimes energy and accumulation will do what grace and delicacy will not. Many of the greatest realistic novelists have been severely criticized for the clumsiness of their prose. In the houses of the stars, too, there are many mansions, and something close to the full range of stylistic varieties may be found in the world of structural fabulation. It is fair to say that no Shakespeare or Joyce has yet appeared in that firmament. But how often have such masters of the warp and woof of English appeared in the past? If to use English as well as Swift or Wells might suffice, then SF has an adequate language already. But many contemporary writers in the field are trying to extend that verbal instrument, and in some cases with considerable success. To sum up—a certain amount of what people "know" about SF without reading it is true—and simply reveals a prejudice against the genre and against other contemporary forms of fiction as well. But much of this "knowledge" is totally unfounded, the result of misinformation and ignorance of the texts themselves.

It is time now to look at some of these texts, both closely and distantly. Let us begin with this passage from a book published in 1971. It is a long passage, and I ask you to consider it seriously as prose, for its rhythms and resonances and for the ideas that it conveys:

He came out into the entrance court and contemplated his bonsai.

Early sun gold-frosted the horizontal upper foliage of the old tree and brought its gnarled limbs into sharp relief, tough brown-gray and crevices of velvet. Only the companion of a bonsai (there are owners of bonsai, but they are a lesser breed) fully understands the relationship. There is an exclusive and individual treeness to the tree because it is a living thing, and living things change, and there are definite ways in which the tree desires to change. A man sees the tree and in his mind makes certain extensions and extrapolations of what he sees, and sets about making them happen. The tree in turn will do only what a tree can do, will resist to the death any attempt to do what it cannot do, or to do it in less time than it needs. The shaping of a bonsai is therefore always a compromise and always a cooperation. A man cannot create a bonsai, nor can a tree; it takes both, and they must understand each other. It takes a long time to do that. One memorizes one's bonsai, every twig, the angle of every crevice and needle, and, lying awake at night or in a pause a thousand miles away, one recalls this or that line or mass, one makes one's plans. With wire and water and light, with tilting and with the planting of water-robbing weeds or heavy root-shading ground cover, one explains to the tree what one wants, and if the explanation is well enough made, and there is great enough understanding, the tree will respond and obey—almost. Always there will be its own self-respecting, highly individual variation: *Very well, I shall do what you want, but I will do it my way.* And for

50

these variations, the tree is always willing to present a clear and logical explanation, and more often than not (almost smiling) it will make clear to the man that he could have avoided it if his understanding had been better.

It is the slowest sculpture in the world, and there is, at times, doubt as to which is being sculptured, man or tree.[1]

This is from a story called "Slow Sculpture" by Theodore Sturgeon. There is no reaching for the purple heights of rhetoric in this passage, but this is not disposable prose, either. It is sculptured prose, spare as a Japanese rock garden, with emphases that owe more to placement and combination than to the qualities of individual words. Sturgeon does not strain the lexicon in search of exotic language, but he puts the words in the right places. Even the paragraphing is thoughtful: a one-sentence paragraph that begins with "He" and ends with "bonsai," then the long paragraph of explanation of the process in which "He" and "bonsai" are involved; and finally another one-sentence paragraph that ends with the words "man or tree." Just consider the structure of this for a moment. In the first sentence we have the personal pronoun "He" and the name "bonsai"—separated by the entire length of that sentence, which is a paragraph. These two terms are separated grammatically as well: "he" is subject; "bonsai" is object. In the last

[1] *Sturgeon Is Alive and Well* (New York: G. P. Putnam's Sons, 1971), p. 73.

51

sentence "He" and "bonsai" have been reduced to their essence: "man" and "tree." They are together in position and in grammatical function. And, semantically, the question of which is the agent and which the patient, which the sculptor and which the sculpture—that question is left open. The construction of these tiny paragraphs functions perfectly to embody the meaning of the message. And the method of embodying this meaning—through placement and function rather than the use of striking words—is perfectly adapted to the subject, which is a kind of gardening that emphasizes placement over selection. Japanese gardening is a semiotic art which communicates powerfully through a careful syntax employing a highly restricted lexicon. Sturgeon's prose works in the same way.

And what is the subject of this text? It is, initially, gardening: the way man and tree interact. But it very easily reaches out to embrace other forms of art. Through the metaphor of gardening as sculpture it considers the question of the artistic process itself. The gardener of words is an artist, too, who works with a medium that works upon him even as he works with it. So this is a text which enables us to see the writing process freshly, too—or any artistic process—as well as to see the treeness of the tree and the manness of the man. And finally, as the whole story makes explicit, this metaphor of slow sculpture is intended to include the ways in which people work upon one another, shaping and being shaped. In the story, this means specifically the way a man and woman come to know and accept each other, but also the way in which any creative man needs to relate to his culture as a whole and the other people around him. A society has its own dynamic, like a bonsai, and the one who would shape it must work in ways as creative and responsive as the ways of a bonsai gardener.

This is all very well, you may say, but is it science fiction? I am not sure. But I know that Theodore Sturgeon is a fine contemporary writer who has never been taken seriously because he is *considered* to be a science fiction writer. And I know that in this particular passage he is clearly, vividly, a structural fabulator. His vision reaches out to embrace more and more structures through this little fable of "He" and "bonsai"—man and tree. If we take literally the metaphor of the willful, thinking tree, we may be able to force the SF label on this passage. But who gives us a license to take this or anything else literally. There is no "literally," only varying intensities of the figurative—remember? Presumably, without Japanese culture the concept of a bonsai would have no literal existence. Trees would exist, and men among them, but this particular form of inter-action might be unheard of. Even now, some readers of a tale like this one may be in doubt as to whether something from the actual world is being described or something fabulous being invented. If

53

Japan did not exist we might all find the notion of a bonsai more fabulous than we do now. But the point is not to classify this story as realism if bonsais exist and as science fiction if they don't— or as fantasy, if the passage is read literally and as fancy if it is taken metaphorically. The point is to recognize that the disposition to structural fabulation is strong here and that the writing is good, whatever the classification. SF is not a watertight generic compartment but an impulse that can manifest itself in many ways. And now it is time to consider some of those ways concretely, by looking at the larger forms of some modern structural fabulations.

Daniel Keyes's *Flowers for Algernon* might be called minimal SF. It establishes only one discontinuity between its world and our own, and this discontinuity requires no appreciable reorientation of our assumptions about man, nature, or society. Yet this break with the normal lifts the whole story out of our familiar experiential situation. It is the thing which enables everything else in the novel, and it is thus crucial to the generation of this narrative and to its affect on readers. How crucial this idea is can be seen in the story's history, which, as it happens, makes an interesting fable in itself. It first appeared as a long story in *The Magazine of Fantasy and Science Fiction* in April 1959. It received a Hugo award in 1960 for the best science fiction novelette of the year. It was then reprinted in *The Best from Fantasy and Sci-*

ence Fiction and in the *Fifth Annual of the Year's Best Science Fiction,* both published in 1960, and in *Best Articles and Stories* and *Literary Cavalcade* in 1961. It was made into a television drama and then rewritten to appear as a full-length novel in 1966. Then it was made into a movie and given, of course, a new title: *CHARLY* (with the *R* childishly reversed). In 1967 it appeared in paperback and has now been through more than thirty printings. My paperback copy, which is from the thirty-second printing (1972), has a scene from the film on the cover, with the word *CHARLY* prominently displayed, and a bundle of "rave" quotations from reviewers on the back cover. Nowhere on the cover of this book does the expression "science fiction" appear. Even the Hugo award (which is at least as reliable an indicator of quality as, say, the Pulitzer Prize for Fiction) goes unmentioned. Inside, in very fine print, the ultra-snoopy purchaser may find in the back pages some words about the author, which indicate that this work first appeared as a "magazine story" (but the name of the magazine is suppressed) and that it won a Hugo award as the "best science novelette" in 1960. Even there, the cautious editors have managed to avoid the stigmatizing expression. *Flowers for Algernon* has gone straight, folks; it has passed the line around the SF ghetto, and to remind us of its sordid history would be downright impolite. And it might chase away a lot of potential customers who "hate science fiction."

An interesting fable, is it not, from which a number of conclusions may be drawn. It certainly reveals something about attitudes toward SF in various quarters, and this is instructive as well as amusing. But it also reveals something about the genre itself. *Flowers for Algernon* could succeed in four distinct forms (novelette, TV drama, full-length film, and full-length novel) because it was based on a powerful concept which worked well in all those forms. Daniel Keyes had an exceptionally good idea for a work of fiction, and the idea is what made it originally and still makes it a work of SF. The idea is simply that an operation might be performed on a severely retarded adult male, which would enable his mind not merely to catch up with those of his peers but actually to surpass theirs. That is half of the idea. The other half, which completes and justifies this idea, is that the effects of the operation would prove impermanent, so that the story involves our watching the protagonist grow into a genius unconsciously, and then consciously but helplessly slip back toward a state of semi-literacy. When this mental voyage has come full circle, the story is over.

For many people, I suspect, the first half of this idea constitutes the domain of SF, a land of inconsequential wish-fulfillment in which the natural laws that constitute the boundaries of human life are playfully suspended. But the best writers of structural fabulation do not settle for mere imaginative play. Daniel Keyes completed the circuit of his idea, and the beauty and power of the resulting story were acknowledged by his readers at the eighteenth World Science Fiction Convention, where he was awarded the Hugo. It should be added that Keyes's execution of his idea was fully adequate to the original conception. He undertook to present the story through a journal kept by the protagonist himself, at the request of his doctor. Thus, we see the growth of Charlie Gordon's mind through the evolution of his prose style as well as in the events narrated. (Mr. Keyes, we might note, happens to be an English teacher). Charlie acquires a competence in grammar, an extensive lexicon, and a rich, vigorous syntax—and then gradually loses all these, as his mental powers fade. He also becomes an impatient, aggressive, arrogant, and unlovable man as his powers increase, inspiring envy, jealousy, and even fear in others. But as he loses his mental competence he regains the affection of those around him—an affection grounded in pity, which is, as Joseph Conrad knew, a form of contempt.

This tale is beautifully problematic. It conveys to us the deprivation involved in mental retardation as no amount of reports or exhortations could possibly do it. And it does this by the fabulative device of an apparently miraculous scientific discovery. It is fabulation that promotes speculation, and speculation that is embodied in an emotionally powerful fable. The intensity of our emotional commitment to the events of any fiction, of course, is a function of countless esthetic choices made by the author—at the level of the word, the sentence, the episode, the character, the ordering of events, and the manner of the presentation. These aspects of *Flowers for Algernon* cannot be dismissed without devoting much more space-time to this story than is available here. I must assert, merely, that Keyes has fleshed out his idea with great skill, and I invite those interested to investigate the text for themselves.

Before moving on to consider another work of SF, however, I should like to use this occasion to examine an aspect of this story which is typical of the genre as a whole, and of the special qualities which seem to differentiate it from other kinds of fiction. Like many works of SF, *Flowers for Algernon* appeared first as a story and then was "expanded" into a novel. Now all of our training in esthetics and all of our background in the critical thought of Flaubert and James, for instance, must lead us to believe that a work of verbal art consists of one set of words in one particular order. Thus, this idea of expansion seems to have more to do with packaging and merchandising than it can do with art. To some extent this must be admitted. The shapes of genres have always had something to do with the means of their communication and the needs of their audiences. But if the "same" story can appear in two different versions just to suit the exigencies of commercial publication as a magazine story and a book, then we may rightfully feel that the work must be deficient in artistic integrity.

This is not a trivial objection, nor is the problem as simple as it seems. James and Flaubert themselves have taught us something about rewriting and revising. All of James's major novels exist in two versions. So do such highly esthetic fictions as Flaubert's *Temptation of Saint Anthony* and Joyce's *A Portrait of the Artist as a Young Man.* James, of course, as a reviser was simply tinkering with his texts stylistically. And Flaubert and Joyce demonstrated their artistic integrity by pruning earlier excesses rather than elaborating and expanding. In fact, they suppressed the early versions entirely. Still, there are many examples, among the classics of narrative literature, of revision which is essentially expansive and sometimes on a grand scale. The later Joyce is expansive as a reviser. Chapters of *Finnegans Wake* often appeared in short versions in magazines and were expanded for inclusion in the book. Faulkner doubled the size of his story "Spotted Horses" when he rewrote it for inclusion in *The Hamlet.* Even Sidney expanded his *Arcadia* immensely in the second version. I mention these instances to indicate that neither revision nor expansion are necessarily esthetic crimes. Nor is there much agreement to the thesis that Faulkner weakened "Spotted Horses" by expanding it—though I would be willing to argue that position myself.

The point is that reappearance in an extended format dictated by the publishing media does not automatically relegate a work to the ranks of esthetic inferiority. Rules will not help us here any more than they will help us resolve other esthetic problems. We must, in the final analysis, examine each case on its merits and decide accordingly. And even within the confines of expanded SF stories, we will find vastly different cases. In *Flowers for Algernon* we have a case in which the basic structure is essentially all there in the short version, and the revision is purely expansive and elaborative. My reaction to reading both versions is that the longer is far superior, because its complications enrich the humanity of the characters, especially Charlie Gordon himself, and because it allows the changes in Charlie to work more gradually. The full-length novel makes the novelette read like a scenario or "treatment," almost, in comparison. But I could not "prove" the long version better than the short. And if it did not exist I might not have felt so strongly the abruptness of the shorter tale. Such problems, though perhaps insoluble, are likely to be of considerable use in the teaching of fiction. A student who compares the two versions of this story is bound to learn something from the experience. And SF provides many similarly instructive situations. In some cases, I should add, the full-length fictions are so changed by their expansion as to constitute entirely new works. Walter M. Miller's *A Canticle for Leibowitz* first saw the light as a short story of no great distinction, though good enough to be anthologized in the fifth annual volume of *Fantasy and Science Fiction.* In book form the *Canticle* undertook to explore whole dimensions of experience and thought which had been unconsidered in the original, altering the idea itself in the process.

In short, because SF depends for its initial impetus on an idea that involves some radical dislocation from present experience, that idea can find expression in varying forms and at variable lengths. But certain formal dimensions will suit the idea better than others, and some formal strategies will not simply develop the idea but will enable it to grow and change in the development. Though rooted in ideas, speculative fabulation is a verbal art like other verbal arts. It is different from other forms of fiction but not so different as we sometimes assume it to be.

If *Flowers for Algernon* is "minimal" SF, in that it treats contemporary life with only a single slight distortion of normal expectations, there are other equally successful works of structural fabulation which insist powerfully on their discontinuities with our contemporary situation. In that form of representational narration which we call fiction, an insistence on discontinuity with normal life must express itself either by emphasizing its representational differences—that is, by showing us different things and creatures from those we know—or by emphasizing its narrational differences from life as we know it—that is, by presenting us with a story more orderly, more meaningful, more extraordinary than those provided by existence. Speculative fabulation, I have been suggesting, is defined

61

by the presence of at least one clear *representational* discontinuity with life as we know it. All fiction—without exception—insists on some *narrational* difference from life; otherwise, it would not be fiction. A story is a story because it organizes existence in a particular narrational way. Realistic writers seek to conceal the fictionality of their fictions. They are embarrassed by the coincidences and other fortuitous conjunctions that their stories require, and they seek to justify them polemically (like Fielding) or to distract our attention from them by narrational complexity (like Joyce). Professed fabulators, on the other hand, have a greater freedom to indulge in extravagant concatenations of events. Still, within the body of modern structural fabulation, we can find an extreme range between those writers who indulge in almost pure speculation and those who adopt an almost pure narration. This range may be illustrated by a brief examination of Olaf Stapledon's *Star Maker* (first published in 1937) and Frank Herbert's *Dune* (1965).

In writing about *Don Quixote,* Lionel Trilling once observed that the first great work in a particular genre may contain "the whole potentiality of the genre." Olaf Stapledon cared too little about storytelling to be called the Cervantes of SF, but if his books could be combined with those of his great contemporary, H. G. Wells, the composite might indeed be said to contain much of the potentiality of the genre. And in particular, no writer has left more ideas to posterity than William Olaf Stapledon. The seeds of other men's novels—and even whole sequences of novels—are to be found in sentences and paragraphs of Stapledon. Thus, I sympathize with the praise of Stapledon, and the anger over his neglect, that we find in Brian Aldiss's recent history of SF, *Billion Year Spree.* Speaking of two of Stapledon's lesser books, Aldiss says they are good things of their kind. Then he returns for a last word on Stapledon's two major fictions:

> But *Last and First Men* and *Star Maker* soar far beyond the accepted limits of science fiction. Or rather, one might say, Stapledon is the great classical example, the cold pitch of perfection as he turns scientific concepts into vast ontological prose poems, the ultimate sf writer. In particular, *Star Maker* stands on that very remote shelf of books which contains huge foolhardy endeavours, carried out according to their author's ambitions. . . . How it is that the funeral masons and morticians who work their preserving processes on Eng. Lit. have rejected Stapledon entirely from their critical incantations is a matter before which speculation falls fainting away. His prose is as lucid as his imagination is huge and frightening. *Star Maker* is really the one great grey holy book of science fiction—perhaps after all there is something appropriate in its wonderful obscurity and neglect![2]

[2] Brian Aldiss, *Billion Year Spree* (Garden City, N.Y.: Doubleday, 1973), p. 208.

63

Star Maker begins simply, with an echo of another cosmic voyage, of which it may be said to be the antitype: "One night when I had tasted bitterness I went out on to the hill." Like an earlier cosmic traveller, Stapledon's nameless narrator achieves in the middle of his life a vision of the universe. And, as Dante's vision was essentially comic because his God cared for man, so Stapledon's is ultimately tragic, because the Star Maker cares only for creation and the critical contemplation of his creatures:

> It was with anguish and horror, and yet with acquiescence, even with praise, that I felt or seemed to feel something of the eternal spirit's temper as it apprehended in one intuitive and timeless vision all our lives. Here was no pity, no proffer of salvation, no kindly aid. Or here were all pity and love, but mastered by a frosty ecstasy. Our broken lives, our loves, our follies, our betrayals, our forlorn and gallant defenses, were one and all calmly anatomized, assessed, and placed. True, they were one and all lived through with complete understanding, with insight and full sympathy, even with passion. But sympathy was not ultimate in the temper of the eternal spirit; contemplation was. And though there was love, there was also hate . . . for there was cruel delight in the comtemplation of every horror, and glee in the downfall of the virtuous. All passions, it seemed, were comprised within the spirit's temper; but mastered, icily gripped within the cold, clear, crystal ecstasy of contemplation.[3]

[3] Olaf Stapledon, *Star Maker* (Baltimore: Penguin Books, 1973), p. 256.

This chilly paragraph comes near the end of *Star Maker,* and the road to it is almost as arduous as Dante's. The man on the hill achieves his final vision by a mental voyage through space-time, which enables him to see an extraordinary number of worlds that are hosts to intelligent forms of life. At first he can move mentally only to worlds which are much like our earth, inhabited by beings whose minds are much like ours. But as he travels his mind acquires companion minds from other worlds, and together they begin to form a composite mind that is capable of a much higher degree of intellection than that of any individual. This composite mind then begins to apprehend the higher orders of intelligence that are abroad in the universe: in time, to understand the stars themselves, and finally to have a vision of the ultimate creative force behind them: the Star Maker. Moving freely in time as well as space, the composite mind first encounters many worlds

> ... in the throes of the same spiritual crisis as that which we knew so well on our native planets. This crisis I came to regard as having two aspects. It was at once a moment in the spirit's struggle to become capable of true community on a world-wide scale; and it was a stage in the age-long task of achieving the right, the finally appropriate, the spiritual attitude toward the universe. (p. 76)

Stapledon describes this common crisis in some of the most moving and important paragraphs in the whole galaxy of speculative fabulation. (Only the pressures of my own space-time and a few last vestiges of common sense prevent me from quoting several pages here, so lovely and so necessary do they seem to me.) He describes worlds which were "always behindhand, always applying old concepts and ideals inappropriately to novel situations." In these worlds "Loud lip-service had been paid to gentleness and tolerance and freedom; but the policy had failed because there was no sincere purpose in it, no conviction of the spirit, no true experience of respect for individual personality." And the passage concludes with an apostrophe to gentleness:

> The highly developed technique of violence threatened to destroy civilization; year by year gentleness lost ground. Few could understand that their world must be saved, not by violence in the short run but by gentleness in the long run. A still fewer could see that, to be effective, gentleness must be a religion; and that lasting peace can never come till the many have wakened to the lucidity of consciousness which, in all these worlds, only the few could as yet attain. (p. 78)

Written in the ominous years when the Second World War was about to begin, these words have unfortunately failed to lose their timeliness and appropriateness. But Stapledon's book is not a jeremiad. His mental traveller sees worlds that succeed as well as worlds that fail. And despite the terrifying Pascalian distances that are traversed, the value of infinitesimal individuality remains uneclipsed. When the traveller returns to his hill and his home, he contemplates "the coming storm" and asks "How to face such an age? How to muster courage, being capable only of homely virtues?" The answers to these questions are contained in the narrative's last paragraph, which looks backward toward all that has been seen and forward toward the continuing human struggle for a dignified existence:

> Two lights for guidance. The first, our little glowing atom of community, with all that it signifies. The second, the cold light of the stars, symbol of the hypercosmical reality, with its crystal ecstasy. Strange that in this light, in which even the dearest love is frostily assessed, and even the possible defeat of our half-waking world is comtemplated without remission of praise, the human crisis does not lose but gains significance. Strange, that it seems more, not less, urgent to play some part in this struggle, this brief effort of animalcules striving to win for their race some increase of lucidity before the ultimate darkness. (p. 262)

To move from Stapledon's *Star Maker* to Herbert's *Dune* is in itself a considerable mental voyage. Where Stapledon is nearly all speculation, Herbert is primarily fabulative. If Stapledon approaches philosophy, Herbert embraces romance. Few would deny that *Dune* is a "great read," as Tolkien's *Lord of the Rings* is a "great read." It gives us strongly defined heroes and villains, engages us in an action which is simple in essence but full of events, twists, complications. *Dune* and its sequel, *Dune Messiah*, first appeared as serial fiction, and they exhibit the frequent climaxes and moments of great suspense which the serial format requires. *Dune is* a romance of adventure, and it is not my intention here to suggest that this romance hides great speculative profundities. What makes it exceptional is the systematic way in which the narrational events are imbedded in a particular ecological setting, and the thoughtfulness and delicacy that have gone into the major characterizations. By choosing as his main location a planet that is naturally a desert, Herbert has alloted the ecosystem a major role in structuring his narrative. And he has developed this role with a wonderful rigor and attention to detail.

This is one great strength of *Dune*. Another is in Herbert's attention to the mechanisms by which religious and political "greatness" are achieved. The imaginary sands of Dune owe a good deal to the real sands of Arabia, and somewhere behind this novel stands T. E. Lawrence's *Seven Pillars of Wisdom*, in which Lawrence speculated on the curious propensity of the semitic geography for producing prophets and mystics. Paul Atreides, who becomes the religious leader Muad'Dib, finds himself cast for the role of prophet in a holy war. Such a situation may lead us to think of things like John Buchan's adventure stories as well as of Lawrence's *Seven Pillars*. But Herbert is saved from operating at the adventure story level—saved by a greater ability to transfer something of actual political maneuvering into narrative form, and to an even greater extent saved by his ability to characterize Paul as a young man who *knows* that he has been cast for a role, that he is enacting a myth with which he is not entirely in sympathy. Like the comic-mythic heroes of John Barth's *Chimera,* Paul Atreides has a powerful sense of the artificiality in his own situation. But where Barth's bumbling heroes struggle to enact their mythic roles fittingly, forcing us to laugh at their comic inepititude, Paul simply takes a sardonic attitude toward "greatness" and tries to ride the mythic whirlwind and tame it for the sake of the people on his adopted planet.

Herbert wisely avoids loading the story with a greater conceptual weight than the romance of adventure can comfortably handle, nor does he often try to philosophize beyond his own intellectual range. He works within the traditional formula, achieving his effects through care and consistency, and through considerable tact in the use of extraordinary mental and physical events. Paul's prophetic powers, for instance, reveal not one future to him, but many possible futures, projections of present history which he may try to actualize or avoid. The other extraordinary mental feats performed by various characters are logical, almost reasonable extensions of the practices of yoga or the possibilities of bio-feedback. Tact, consistency, and restraint are what make this adventure story an exceptionally mature and interesting one. And nowhere do these qualities emerge more clearly than in Herbert's presentation of the ecology of Dune and the various human responses to that ecology. Here he is most structural, most aware of system and necessity, and this awareness is the backbone of the book.

With *Dune* and *Star Maker* I have tried to illustrate something of the extreme ranges of structural fabulation. Different as they are, they share a willingness to leap from the world as we know it to other and quite different worlds. They are not concerned to justify these voyages scientifically or to present them as extrapolations of present existence, but in their different ways they illuminate aspects of our contemporary human situation: *Star Maker* being profoundly cognitive, and *Dune* being mainly sublimative but drawing strength from its cognitive dimension. There is, however, another major development of contemporary SF, which is much more tightly tied to our immediate situation in space and time. Some of the strongest and most valuable of structural fabulations are direct projections of the present, which provide concrete realizations of current trends in our political and social situations. These projections vary interestingly with the distance from the present that they assume, as our ability to distinguish the natural from the supernatural diminishes with movement away from present space-time. In fact, it is possible to recognize two distinct classes of contemporary SF, according to whether their events are located near our present situation or far away in time or space. This is not a continuum along which works are spread equally from one end to another, but something more like magnetic polarization, in which a cluster of quite different kinds of fiction has formed itself around each pole.

In crude spatiotemporal terms we have one set of works which definitely take place on our earth and within a century (usually within a half century) or so of the date of composition. And there is another set of works which are set in places remote from us in space or time—centuries or light years away. Some of the most powerful and cognitively useful works of SF have been projections into the near future, like Orwell's *1984*, Zamyatin's *We*, and Anthony Burgess's *Clockwork Orange* and *The Wanting Seed*. As *Flowers for Algernon* indicates, such novels may emphasize the personal over the social, but this is unusual. This form is marked by its emphasis on social questions. Taken together, these fictions of the near future represent a continuation of the traditions of sociological and psychological fiction, or a merging of that tradition with the older tradition of Utopian fabulation. They are projections of realism and naturalism into future time. Thus, while fictions of the far future or of distant locations take a stance which is either philosophically speculative or romantically sublimative, these fictions of the near future draw their power from the cognitive systems of present social science. They are in some sense predictive rather than merely speculative, and they predict on the basis of current knowledge in the fields of political science, economics, psychology, sociology, and the other human sciences. Such fictions often attain great emotional power in a very interesting way. They present a noticeable discontinuity with our current situation—but they insist that this altered situation is *not* actually discontinuous, that it is in fact a reasonable projection of existing trends. These fictions of the near future thus deny that they are discontinuous, while nevertheless shocking us by their difference from the world that—whether we claim to like it or not—we are presently functioning in reasonably well or we would be in no position to be reading this literature at all.

The contemporary novelist who is preeminent in this field is as yet far too little known outside the narrow circle of SF readership. His name is John Brunner; he is the author of an astonishing number of quickie space operas; and he has written two extraordinary novels of the near future: *Stand on Zanzibar* (which won a Hugo in 1969) and *The Sheep Look Up* (which appeared in paperback in November 1973). In a crude way we can designate *Stand on Zanzibar* an overpopulation novel and *The Sheep Look Up* a pollution novel. In each book one aspect of the present human dilemma is projected into the near future, a future in which it has become the dominant cultural force. Brunner's technique in these books is reminiscent of that used by the giants of naturalism. Like Zola, he

72

handles crowds and mobs with an almost cinematic power. Like the Dos Passos of *U.S.A.* he covers an extraordinary amount of territory and intersperses items from the mass media among the events and situations of his narrative (only, these quotations are usually fictions, projections, models, rather than documents—in the future facts must be invented). We follow groups of characters along separate paths which illustrate aspects of a richly imagined and developed cultural situation. The documentary plausibility of these novels is staggering. In the series of ecological disasters which are combined in *The Sheep Look Up,* there is not one which lacks its firmly planted root in our present mode of existence. Brunner's strength is not in the deeply individuated characterizations of the psychological novel but in a superbly controlled plausibility and typicality. These are large, dense books which weigh upon us with the oppressive gravity of all-too-plausible nightmares. The characters in these fictions are as trapped by their cultural systems as the characters of Zola and Dreiser, only these systems are not those presently in existence but are speculative projections of the present.

Something strange and wonderful happens to naturalism when it is projected in this way. We do not merely experience the depression of sharing the lives of beings trapped and betrayed by the laws of social and physiological existence. Instead we feel, along with sympathy for these stifled and twisted lives, the exhilarating thought that this *is,* after all, a projection, not an actuality. This future, however plausible, is not inevitable. We can *do* something about it, now, before it is too late. These two novels of Brunner's are educative as only fictions of the near future can be. They force upon us the consequences of our present behavior with a power which no other form of discourse can hope to equal.

In my first lecture, I spoke of the necessity for future-fiction. Let me reiterate that thought in this context. We human beings in highly technological countries are making decisions now that will have inevitable consequences for our children and grandchildren. If we persist in thinking only in terms of our present needs we will leave to these descendants a veritable hell on earth. But how can we avoid this? How can we think of mankind as extending in space beyond the boundaries of our own national interests and in time beyond the boundaries of our own generation? Our governments seem incapable of breaking the circle of chauvinism that surrounds them. In many cases they are more concerned with their own survival in the seats of power than with the well-being of their people. They can't or won't think beyond the next election or the next party congress. The mass media can tell us only of the present, and of that they can capture only those aspects which fit their highly reductive formulae for news and information. If we are to break the circle of indifference and act in accordance with a structural perception of the uni-

74

verse, we shall have to depend on the lonely voices of imaginative human beings to bring home to us the implications of our actions. To live well in the present, to live decently and humanely, *we must see into the future.* And if the people as a whole are to accept the present sacrifices required to enable a bearable future to exist, then they must be made aware of the living reality of the unbearable futures that we must avoid. Those of us privileged by our education to have any sense of the awfulness of our situation are in the position of Sturgeon's man with the bonsai. We must try to work a slow sculpture on our world. No government can save us if the people do not want to be saved.

I am not very hopeful about our ability to rise above present selfishness and direct our culture toward a decent human future. But if there is any hope at all, it will depend on the ability of our men and women of imagination to make us see and feel the reality of our situation and the consequences of our present actions. Truly, where there is no vision, the people perish.

4

The Good Witch of the West

IT SHOULD BE CLEAR BY NOW THAT IN THESE LEC-
tures I have not been trying to say the last word on
the subject of structural fabulation but to provide
a kind of framework for the study of this flourish-
ing branch of modern fiction. Thus, in the first two
lectures I tried to produce a sketch or model of our
cultural situation and of the system of literary
genres as it is presently constituted—in order to
show how what we loosely designate "science fiction" answers to our present cultural and literary
needs. Then, in the third lecture I presented some
examples that illustrate the range of this modern
kind of speculative narration: first, the two ex-
tremes, the highly cognitive but barely narrative
Star Maker of Stapledon, and the powerfully sublimative but marginally cognitive *Dune;* then, the
more rigorously extrapolative social projections of
John Brunner, *Stand on Zanzibar* and *The Sheep
Look Up.* These works describe a kind of triangle,
bounded by philosophy (Stapledon), history

(Brunner), and romance (Herbert)—forms of discourse that have been with us for a long time. Each of these three kinds of structural fabulation has its own special strengths and also its potential weaknesses, which writers may or may not succeed in avoiding. If speculation itself becomes too dominant, a work may lose its fictional power, and even Stapledon, great as he is, has suffered from this very weakness. If romance dominates a work too powerfully, it loses cognitive value and fails to maintain a place in the literary system of adult readers. Tolkien, it seems to me, accepts this limitation, though he romances beautifully. Finally, if a work becomes too enmeshed in historical data and commentary, whether recorded or invented, it may fail in narrative interest—and this is a problem which John Brunner has had to face, though I would argue that he has largely solved it.

The other dimension of structural fabulation considered in the third lecture was that of language. Clearly, for any fictional work to succeed, its language must be adequate to its overall design. And here, though admitting that in the world of structural fabulation ideas take precedence over their verbal formulae, I tried to indicate that writers like Sturgeon, Keyes, and Stapledon himself use language with a care and precision that is more than functional and approaches beauty—as any functional work done carefully and economically approaches beauty.

Now, having done all this to illustrate aspects of

78

the range and quality of structural fabulation, I may have inadvertently given the impression that no writers come close to putting it all together. This is, most emphatically, not the case. Though it is appropriate to recognize that some writers work with minimal distortion of contemporary probabilities and project carefully into the near future, while others move into much more distant territory, within each of these areas there are certain writers who have succeeded in blending speculation and narration superbly. The near-future projections of Zamyatin, Orwell, Huxley, Burgess, Sturgeon, and Brunner, for instance, all solve their artistic problems with considerable success. And in the more fabulous reaches of space-time Wells, Clarke, Asimov, Heinlein, Herbert, Zelazny, and Delaney (among others) have recorded notable successes. But if I were to choose one writer to illustrate the way in which it is possible to unite speculation and fabulation in works of compelling power and beauty, employing a language that is fully adequate to this esthetic intention, that writer would be the Good Witch of the West.

In the Land of Oz, all the good witches come from the north and south, the wicked witches from the east and west. But we do not live in the Land of Oz and must take our witches as we find them. Ursula Kroeber Le Guin, born in California and a resident of Oregon, is very much of the west, and the literary magic she works is so dazzling as to make the title of "good witch" almost literally appropriate. (And perhaps I should add that the one photograph of her that I have seen pictures a woman of an appropriate formidability.) Since 1966 she has published nine novels, three of them designed especially for younger readers, and all of them likely to appear in the section reserved for science fiction and fantasy in your neighborhood bookstore. She has been compared to C. S. Lewis, with some appropriateness, especially as concerns her juvenile trilogy, but that comparison fails ultimately because she is a better writer than Lewis: her fictions, both juvenile and adult, are richer, deeper, and more beautiful than his. She is probably the best writer of speculative fabulation working in this country today, and she deserves a place among our major contemporary writers of fiction. For some writers, the SF ghetto serves a useful protective function, preserving them from comparison with their best contemporaries. For Ursula Le Guin, as for others, this protection, and the sense of a responsive, relatively uncritical audience that goes with it, may have been helpful during her early development as a writer. But with *The Left Hand of Darkness* (1969) she displayed powers so remarkable that only full and serious critical scrutiny can begin to reveal her value as a writer. It is my intention here to initiate such scrutiny, concentrating on that excellent novel but glancing also at her other fiction, especially at the first volume of her trilogy for young people.

80

The Earthsea trilogy consists of *A Wizard of Earthsea* (1968), *The Tombs of Atuan* (1971), and *The Farthest Shore* (1972). These books have been compared to C. S. Lewis's chronicles of Narnia, especially by English reviewers, for whom this constitutes considerable praise. But the comparison is misleading. Lewis's books are allegories in the narrow sense of that much abused word—his Lion *is* Christ, and the whole structure of the chronicles is a reenactment of Christian legend. The fundamental story is fixed, and the narrative surface becomes simply a new way of clothing that story and retelling it as a heroic adventure. The ultimate value of such allegorizing, then, must reside in the permanent value of the legendary pattern itself, raising the question of how the story of Christ functions cognitively to help us understand our world and live in it. My own feeling in this matter is that Lewis's narratives work on us because we are preconditioned to be moved by that particular material, with its legend of a redemptive sacrifice— preconditioned by our particular cultural heritage rather than by the shape of the world itself. In other words, this kind of allegory is leading its readers toward a stock response based on a pre-established and rigidly codified set of values. But there is another kind of allegory—allegory in a broader sense—which is more speculative and less dogmatic. Ursula Le Guin, in the Earthsea trilogy, relies on the mythic patterns of sin and redemption, quest and discovery, too, but she places them in the service of a metaphysic which is entirely responsible to modern conditions of being because its perspective is broader than the Christian perspective—because finally it takes the world more seriously than the Judeo-Christian tradition has ever allowed it to be taken.

What Earthsea represents, through its world of islands and waterways, is the universe as a dynamic, balanced system, not subject to the capricious miracles of any diety, but only to the natural laws of its own working, which include a role for magic and for powers other than human, but only as aspects of the great Balance or Equilibrium, which is the order of this cosmos. Where C. S. Lewis worked out of a specifically Christian set of values, Ursula Le Guin works not with a theology but with an ecology, a cosmology, a reverence for the universe as a self-regulating structure. This seems to me more relevant to our needs than Lewis, but not simply because it is a more modern view—rather because it is a deeper view, closer to the great pre-Christian mythologies of this world and also closer to what three centuries of science have been able to discover about the nature of the universe. No one, in fact, has ever made magic seem to function so much like science as Ursula Le Guin— which is perhaps why it is no gross error to call her work science fiction, and also why the term *science fiction* seems finally inadequate to much of the material it presently designates in our bookstores and other rough and ready categorizations.

A Wizard of Earthsea is the story of the making of a mage, the education and testing of a young man born with the power to work wonders but lacking the knowledge to bring this power to fruition and to control its destructive potential. Ged's education is begun by his first master, Ogion, on his home island of Gont. This education continues and becomes more formal when he studies at the School for Wizards on Roke. What he learns there is manifold, but much of it is contained in this one speech by the gentle instructor in illusion, the Master Hand:

> "This is a rock; *tolk* in the True Speech," he said, looking mildly up at Ged now. "A bit of the stone of which Roke Isle is made, a little bit of the dry land on which men live. It is itself. It is part of the world. By the Illusion-Change you can make it look like a diamond—or a flower or a fly or an eye or a flame—" The rock flickered from shape to shape as he named them and returned to rock. "But that is mere seeming. Illusion fools the beholder's senses; it makes him see and hear and feel that the thing is changed. But it does not change the thing. To change this rock into a jewel, you must change its true name. And to do that, my son, even to so small a scrap of the world, is to change the world. It can be done. Indeed it can be done. It is the art of the Master Changer, and you will learn it when you are ready to learn it. But you must not change one thing, one pebble, one grain of sand, until you know what good

83

and evil will follow on that act. The world is in balance, in Equilibrium. A wizard's power of Changing and of Summoning can shake the balance of the world. It is dangerous, that power. It is most perilous. It must follow knowledge and serve need. To light a candle is to cast a shadow. . . ."[1]

To be a wizard is to learn the "true names" of things. But the number of things in the world, the difficulty of discovering their names, set limits to magical power, even as the boundaries of scientific knowledge set limits to the power of science. As the Master Namer puts it,

"Thus, that which gives us the power to work magic, sets the limits of that power. A mage can control only what is near him, what he can name exactly and wholly. And this is well. If it were not so, the wickedness of the powerful or the folly of the wise would long ago have sought to change what cannot be changed, and Equilibrium would fail. The unbalanced sea would overwhelm the islands where we perilously dwell, and in the old silence all voices and all names would be lost."(p. 61)

Finally, the greater knowledge, the greater the limitations—a view which is voiced by the Master Summoner after Ged has abused his youthful powers and unleashed a shadow of terror into the world:

"You thought, as a boy, that a mage is one who can do anything. So I thought, once. So did we all. And the truth is that as a man's real power grows and his knowledge widens, ever the way he can follow grows narrower:

[1] *A Wizard of Earthsea* (New York: Ace Books, 1968), pp. 56-57.

until at last he chooses nothing, but does only and wholly what he *must do.* . . ." (pp. 86-87)

Ged's quest, after his recovery (for the shadow wounded him gravely), is to find the shadow and subdue it, to restore the Balance that he has upset by working his power in a way beyond his knowledge. His quest is both an adventure story and an allegory which clearly raises the parallel to Lewis's Narnian allegory. For Ged must try to redeem his world, too. He must struggle with an evil power and suffer in the process. The difference is that Ged himself is the sinner who has made this redemption necessary. In C. S. Lewis's universe, which is the traditional Christian universe, God functions like Maxwell's demon, to distort the natural balance of the universe. God accepts the blame for man's sin without accepting the responsibility, leaving the world forever unbalanced, with man forever burdened by a debt that cannot be repaid. In the case of Ged, however, the redemption of the individual will restore the Great Balance, making the world harmonious again. Ged's final sacrifice will save both himself and the world equally, and at once. There is no eternity, no heaven in this universe, though the spirits of the dead are not lost; there is only the balance, in which death defines life as the darkness defines the light.

Ged's magic is useless to him against the shadow, because he does not know its true name, while it knows his. Finally, it is through an exercise of intuitive logic that he determines the shadow's name. Knowing how it knows his name, he then knows its:

> Aloud and clearly, breaking that old silence, Ged spoke the shadow's name, and in the same moment the shadow spoke without lips or tongue, saying the same word: "Ged." And the two voices were one voice.. (p. 201)

The shadow was himself, his own capacity for evil, summoned up by his own power. To become whole, he had to face it, name it with his own name, and accept it as a part of himself. Thus by restoring the balance in himself, he helped to restore the balance of his world. The poetry of this balance shines through Ged's words, which are Ursula Le Guin's, as he explains the sources of power to a little girl.

> "It is no secret. All power is one in source and end, I think. Years and distances, stars and candles, water and wind and wizardry, the craft in a man's hand and the wisdom in a tree's root: they all arise together. My name and yours, and the true name of the sun, or a spring of water, or an unborn child, all are syllables of the great word that is very slowly spoken by the shining of the stars. There is no other power. No other name." (p. 185)

Is this magic? Religion? Science? The great gift of Ursula Le Guin is to offer us a perspective in which these all merge, in which realism and fantasy are not opposed, because the supernatural is naturalized—not merely postulated but regulated, systematized, made part of the Great Equilibrium itself. And of course, this is also art, in which the sounds of individual sentences are as cunningly balanced as the whole design, in which a great allegory of the destructive power of science unleashed, and a little allegory of an individual seeking to conquer his own chaotic impulses, come together as neatly as the parts of a dove's tail. If Ursula Le Guin had written nothing but her three books for young people, her achievement would be secure, but she has done much more, capped, for the present, by her extraordinary accomplishment in *The Left Hand of Darkness,* which in its complexity and maturity shows what in the trilogy makes those books juvenile. It is not simply that their style is legendary, and it is certainly not that their world is falsified or prettified in any condescending way. It is simply that in such a world of substance and essence all cultural and social complications are stripped to the bone. In her most mature work, Ursula Le Guin shows us how speculative fabulation can deal with the social dimensions of existence as adequately as the most "realistic" of traditional models—or perhaps more adequately in some important respects. For she does not present us with the details of a social chronicle but raises questions about the nature of social organization itself. She is not so much a sociologist as a structural anthropologist, dealing with the principles rather than the data of social organization. Her method, of course, is distinctly fictional, fabulative, constructive. She offers us a

87

model world deliberately altered from the world we know, so as to reveal to us aspects of the "known" that have escaped our notice.

The concepts that rule the construction of *The Left Hand of Darkness* are those of likeness and unlikeness, native and alien, male and female. The questions asked are about the ways that biology, geology, and social history control our perception of the world and our actions in it. The convention of representation adopted in this novel is one of the most fundamental—in some hands the most hackneyed—of the SF tradition: the alien encounter. The first stirrings of speculative fabulation were marked by stories of voyages to strange lands with different customs, and these were answered later by reciprocal tales of strangers from China or Mars or Wherehaveyou visiting our Western world. Such fictions have always offered opportunities for the distortion of habitual perspective that enables cognition—and not merely recognition—to take place. In some hands the merely monstrous aspects of the alien encounter have been emphasized. In others, the eyes of narrator and author have become so bemused by the new social spectacle that narrative development virtually disappears, yielding to description and meditation. In many the observer, who is usually the narrator, becomes a mere eye, losing all personality, even all fleshly attributes, in the process. One of the sources of Jonathan Swift's undying power is his refusal to allow Gulliver to become a bodiless eye. And the sources of Ursula Le Guin's achievement in *The Left Hand of Darkness* lie in her ability to maintain a powerful narrative interest in characters who grow richer and more interesting to the very last words of the book and who themselves embody the larger problems and ideas that are being investigated.

The events of the novel take place on a remote planet in a corner of the known universe, at a time in the distant future when our earth, Terra, is just one of many earths or inhabited planets, in many solar systems, organized by a quasi-governmental body called the Ekumen. This planet, Gethen, was first called Winter by observers from the Ekumen secretly landed upon it because it is experiencing an ice age similar to those Earth experienced in the remote past. As the novel begins, a single ambassador from the Ekumen has landed openly on the planet, seeking to encourage the various countries on Gethen to join one another in establishing a trade and cultural exchange with the rest of the known universe. All the action in the novel takes place in two countries: Karhide, which is essentially feudal in its social and political systems, and Orgoreyn, which has a bureaucratic government something like a modern totalitarian state. In both countries all forms of social and personal life are affected by the sub-arctic weather patterns and by the one physical feature which distinguishes Gethenians from all other known human beings: their peculiar sexuality.

The Gethenians are all bisexual or hermaphroditic, but their sexuality is periodic, like estrus in animals, rather than continual, as in human beings. In a periodic monthly cycle they come into a brief period of heat or "kemmer," in which they experience a sexual drive much stronger than the human and then return to a-sexuality for the bulk of the month. All Gethenians have both male and female sexual equipment, and it is a matter of chance which organs become activated during their kemmering, the activation resulting from a couple's touching so that each couple becomes a hetero-sexual pair, but not always in the same way. Thus every person may become a father or a mother, and between periods of kemmer will not be either one sex or the other but something neutrally located between the two. One of the first secret investigators of Gethen reported on this as follows:

> The fact that everyone between seventeen and thirty-five or so is liable to be ... "tied down to childbearing," implies that no one is quite so thoroughly "tied down" here as women, elsewhere, are likely to be—psychological-ly or physically. Burden and privilege are shared out pretty equally; everybody has the same risk to run or choice to make. Therefore nobody here is quite so free as a free male anywhere else. ... When you meet a Gethenian you cannot and must not do what a bisexual naturally does, which is to cast him in the role of Man or Woman, while adopting toward him a corresponding role depen-dent on your expectations of the patterned or possible interactions between persons of the same or the opposite sex. Our entire pattern of socio-sexual interaction is

nonexistent here. They cannot play the game. They do not see one another as men or women. This is almost impossible for our imagination to accept. What is the first question we ask about a new-born baby?[2]

I submit that such a deliberate variation on human sexuality can help us to see the realities of our own sexual situation more clearly, and to feel them more deeply, than any non-imaginative work of sociology or "realistic" fiction. But this is only a beginning. This passage is couched in the clear but impersonal language of a trained social observer. It *is* sociology, though fictional. But this voice is only heard once in the novel, and it is one among a half dozen distinct voices through which we apprehend the world of Winter. We hear the bardic voices of folk-tellers, the cryptic voices of religious mysticism, and above all we hear the voices of the two main characters, who draw our human concern more intensely as the story progresses. One is the voice of Genly Ai, the Mobile or ambassador of the Ekumen to Gethen. The other is that of Therem Harth rem ir Estraven, one of the few men on Gethen with the foresight and imagination to accept the ambassador for what he is and seek to aid him in his mission. On one level, the story is the story of Ai's mission, his attempt to bring Gethen into the Ekumen, with Estraven's assistance. On another, it is simply the story of two human

[2] *The Left Hand of Darkness* (New York: Ace Books, 1972), pp. 93-94.

beings, two aliens, seeking to communicate with one another through cultural and biological barriers. On the level of the mission this is an exciting story, but not more so than many other works of science fiction. On the personal level, this is a richer and more moving tale than most. But the great power of the book comes from the way it interweaves all its levels and combines all its voices and values into an ordered, balanced, whole. In the end, everything is summed up in the relationship between the two main characters, and the narrative is shaped to present this relationship with maximum intensity.

Estraven, wrongly declared a traitor in his native land of Karhide, rescues Genly Ai from an Orgota concentration camp, where he is on the point of death. Together they flee nearly a thousand miles across the glacierized cap of the planet, toward a problematic safety. Isolated in this way, they must learn to understand one another truly or die, the mission they have both sacrificed so much for dying with them. This situation in this setting would challenge any writer's ability to describe a natural scene so stark and so important, to narrate an adventure so simple and physical, and at the same time to deepen the characterization of the adventurers rather than allow their personalities to be overwhelmed by the awesome scenery and the power of the adventurous trek itself. For Ursula Le Guin this challenge becomes an opportunity to bring together the main concerns of the work.

Against Winter's most wintry aspect a human and cultural drama is brought into high relief. The adventure is presented alternately through the final report of Genly Ai to the Ekumen and the journal kept by Estraven for his family. And each of them tells the story of their struggle with the elements and their coming to know and accept one another. As Estraven puts it, looking back at their past misunderstandings before they begin their trek: "Mr. Ai, we've seen the same events with different eyes." But where this earlier had led only to blurred focus and confusion, by the end of the novel it gives to both of them a depth of perception that neither could have attained alone.

Here is the way Estraven sees his companion:

> There is a frailty about him. He is all unprotected, exposed, vulnerable, even to his sexual organ which he must carry always outside himself; but he is strong, unbelievably strong. I am not sure he can keep hauling any longer than I can, but he can haul harder and faster than I—twice as hard. He can lift the sledge at front or rear to ease it over an obstacle. I could not lift and hold that weight. . . . To match his frailty and strength, he has a spirit easy to despair and quick to defiance: a fierce impatient courage. (p. 216)

This is, of course, simply the description of a manly man, who seems mercurial to one who maintains a placid, sexless perspective. On another occasion, the envoy is close to tears, and Estraven notices this:

93

He looked ready to cry but did not. I believe he considers crying either evil or shameful. Even when he was very ill and weak, the first days of our escape, he hid his face from me when he wept. Reasons personal, racial, social, sexual—how can I guess why Ai must not weep? Yet his name is a cry of pain. For that I first sought him out in Erhenrang, a long time ago it seems now; hearing talk of "an Alien" I asked his name, and heard for answer a cry of pain from a human throat across the night. (p. 218)

And finally, coming into the period of kemmer, with its heightened sexuality, the Gethenian contemplates the other:

The trouble is of course, that he is, in his curious fashion, also in kemmer: always in kemmer. A strange lowgrade sort of desire it must be, to be spread out over every day of the year and never to know the choice of sex but there it is; and here am I. . . . After all he is no more an oddity, a sexual freak, than I am: up here on the ice each of us is singular, isolate, I as cut off from those like me, from my society and its rules, as he is from his. There is no world full of other Gethenians here to explain and support my existence. We are equals at last, equal, alien, and alone. (p. 221)

And from his alien perspective Genly Ai comes finally to perceive Estraven in a new way, and to accept his difference:

And I saw then again, and for good, what I had always been afraid to see, and had pretended not to see in him: that he was a woman as well as a man. Any need to explain the sources of that fear vanished with the fear;

94

what I was left with was, at last, acceptance of him as he really was. Until then I had rejected him, refused him his own reality. He had been quite right to say that he, the only person on Gethen who trusted me, was the only Gethenian I distrusted. For he was the only one who had entirely accepted me as a human being: who had liked me personally and given me entire personal loyalty: and who therefore had demanded of me an equal degree of recognition, of acceptance. I had not been willing to give it. I had been afraid to give it. I had not wanted to give my trust, my friendship to a man who was a woman, a woman who was a man. (p. 234)

They come together then as friends, though not sexually, for, as Ai puts it, "for us to meet sexually would be for us to meet once more as aliens. We had touched, in the only way we could touch." And they remain friends until death parts them, Ai and Therem, I and Thou.

So truly does Genly Ai enter into the worldview of his friend, that when his mission finally succeeds, and members of his own species, friends whom he has known before, land on Gethen, he finds their alien presence overpowering:

Out they came, and met the Karhiders with a beautiful courtesy. But they all looked strange to me, men and women, well as I knew them. Their voices sounded strange: too deep, too shrill. They were like a troupe of great, strange animals, of two different species: great apes with intelligent eyes, all of them in rut, in kemmer. . . . They took my hand, touched me, held me. (p. 279)

95

After this he retires to his room and is soothed by a Gethenian physician: "His quiet voice and his face, a young, serious face, not a man's face and not a woman's, a human face, these were a relief to me, familiar, right." We may remember Gulliver here, in the stable talking to his horses, and this may lead us to smile. But this scene is still a touching and a meaningful one. It leads us away from Swift's hatred of the bestial in man and toward a love of the world's possibilities for intelligent life. This meaning is reinforced in the last lines of the book. The envoy visits the parent and child of his dead friend on their ancestral estate, to bring them the story of the great adventure, and the book closes with the words of young Estraven, which are full of the same generosity of spirit and openness to life that had made Therem so remarkable:

> "I should like to hear that tale, my Lord Envoy," said old Esvans, very calm. But the boy, Therem's son, said stammering, "Will you tell us how he died?—Will you tell us about the other worlds out among the stars—the other kinds of men, the other lives?" (p. 283)

This eagerness for the future, this willingness to embrace the Other, is surely a major force in all science fiction, though it has seldom been presented with such eloquence as in this book. And it is as surely something we need, to face the future ourselves. We need also the ultimate wisdom of *The Left Hand of Darkness* about the nature of opposition, which is the extreme form of otherness. An experience of Ai and Therem on the ice

brings this wisdom home to them and to us. At one
point a curious cloud cover arises, leaving them in a
hazy light but taking away color and shadow. In
this white world they cannot continue on their
way, can barely maintain balance, and can scarcely
perceive the crevasses that threaten them with
death. When they stop and make camp, Ai com-
plains of his own fear, and Therem replies, "Fear's
very useful. Like darkness. Like shadows. . . . It's
queer that daylight's not enough. We need the
shadows, in order to walk" (pp. 251-252). And Ai
thinks of a Gethenian folk poem, the Lay of
Tomer, which Estraven had recited for him, and of
a symbol which has had a history on many worlds.
He borrows Estraven's journal and draws the symbol on one of its pages, explaining,

> "It's found on Earth, and on Hain-Davenant, and on
> Chiffewar. It's yin and yang. *Light is the left hand of
> darkness* . . . how did it go? Light, dark. Fear, courage.
> Cold, warmth. Female, male. It is yourself, Therem.
> Both and one. A shadow on snow." (p. 252)

As in the Earthsea narratives, Ursula Le Guin
remains the poet of the Great Balance, but here the
balance as a tension, an opposition like the halves
of an arch, is emphasized. "To oppose is to maintain," Estraven says, and so says the creator of
Estraven. Thus male is defined by female and female by male, light by darkness and darkness by
light. As the Master Hand said on Roke, "To light a
candle is to make a shadow." And thus for us to
see what it is to be human, as opposed to merely

male or female, we need a non-human shadow, a world other than our own. And this is the value of the harmless illusion worked by this Mistress of Fiction in *The Left Hand of Darkness.* The book contains far more riches than I have been able to consider here—in fact I have left whole aspects of it unconsidered, but this discussion should serve to suggest what kind of book it is and what kind of writer its author has become. I have ignored also, her four previous adult novels, which, though no one has quite the completeness and complexity of this one, are able and interesting fictions, especially *Planet of Exile,* in which the encounter of alien races is particularly well managed, though now we may see this merely as preparation for the bigger book which followed. Her most recent novel, *The Dispossessed,* is a rich and remarkable work of utopian speculation—one of the most satisfying fictions ever achieved in that ancient and difficult speculative genre. With each book she writes, Ursula K. Le Guin places us more deeply in her debt.

One danger in using works or writers illustratively, as I have done throughout these lectures, is that each inclusion excludes so many alternate possibilities. Though I consider Ursula K. Le Guin at the very top of the group of contemporary structural fabulators, there are many other writers whose achievements approach hers, and whom I have virtually ignored here. I apologize for that and hope to offer some compensation in the list of titles included in the bibliography. But this fictional genre is so alive and active that no bibliographer can hope to keep up with it. And this is fine, this is what contemporary literature should be—at least one jump ahead of the critics. So I conclude by urging readers to investigate this rich and fruitful territory and experience for themselves the joy and excitement of discovery. And I urge my fellow teachers and makers of curricula to open their courses to the literature of structural fabulation and allow it to contribute to that critical revaluation of our literary past which functions so powerfully to keep that past alive.

Afterword

SOME TYING TOGETHER OF THINGS MAY BE IN order, here, though I would hesitate to seek a "conclusion" to a study necessarily so open-ended as this one. First, a review of terminology may be useful. And second, some discussion of problems raised by this terminology itself and the concepts it attempts to signify. In the course of these lectures I have at times accepted the traditional Anglo-Saxon distinction between romance and realism, and have at times rejected it. This needs some clarification. The distinction itself was made by an empirically oriented race in an age of developing empiricism Thus, it must have some value, if only a historical one. The distinction was originally and has been traditionally invidious, with realism being the privileged form. This suited a materialistic and positivistic age, and the science of that age seemed to lend support to a realistic notion of the cosmos. But science has become increasingly removed from the world of common sense, increasingly imaginative and "unrealistic" in its search for the true structure of the cosmos, and this has ultimately strengthened the potential of didactic romance or fabulation as a form of cognitive fiction—thus striking at the roots of the very notion of "realism." That modern body of fictional works which we loosely designate "science fiction" either accepts or pretends to accept a cognitive responsibility to imagine what is not yet apparent or existent, and to examine this in some systematic way. The acceptance of this responsibility by a writer capable of measuring up to it leads to what I have called structural fabulation.

Seen in cultural terms, then, structural fabulation is a kind of narrative which is genuinely fictional but strongly influenced by modern science. It is specifically romantic in that it breaks, consciously and deliberately, with what we know or accept to be the case. But it develops its arbitrary parameters with a rigor and consistency that imitates in its fictional way the rigor of scientific method. Seen in purely formal terms, structural fabulation is a development of a tradition of speculative fabulation that has a long history in Western culture. This tradition itself is rooted in the genre of didactic romance, and can be seen as a dialectical antithesis of dogmatic fabulation. This whole history can be seen in the diagram on page 103.

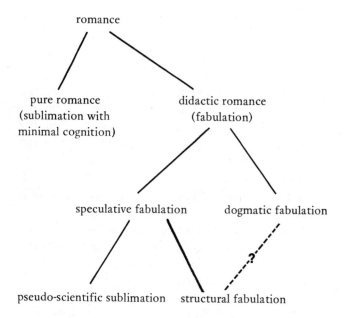

Perhaps the most crucial question or objection raised in the debates initiated by these lectures has involved the status of structural fabulation with respect to dogma. To some critics I have seemed to invoke a new orthodoxy and to preach a new dogma called structuralism, thus establishing for structural fabulation a kind of religious sanction based on science. There is a certain amount of truth in this charge, and I have acknowledged this by the dotted line with the question mark in the diagram. Can speculation be evaluated for truth-value and still be speculative? Can we ask for rigor without insisting on dogma? Can we expect the imagination to be regulated by something unimaginative without stifling creativity itself? Great questions—with social as well as literary implications. And I have no easy answers for them. I hope and believe these questions can be answered in the affirmative. Partly because our science itself must be speculative in order to continue. And even more because fabulation is *not* a science. It does not ask "What is?" It asks "What if?" And by doing so it forces us to think about what is and what may be. The surge of pleasure we get when we begin to read any new work of science fiction comes through the lift off from our land of Is into the land of May Be. But the final joy of structural fabulation, as Ursula Le Guin shows us so beautifully in her new book, *The Dispossessed,* comes not from the departure, nor even from the trip itself, but from the return. As an aging dogmatist once said,

> We shall not cease from exploration
> And the end of all our exploring
> Will be to arrive where we started
> And know the place for the first time.

Select Bibliography

This is a list of places to start. Rather than reprint here checklists available elsewhere, I have preferred to name a few basic texts which will themselves lead to all the others.

Clareson, Thomas D.
Science Fiction Criticism: An Annotated Checklist. Kent, Ohio: Kent State Press, 1972.

> This is an indispensable volume for the serious student of SF. It is thorough, orderly, and immensely useful. Its eighth section provides a bibliography of other checklists and bibliographies.

Aldiss, Brian
Billion Year Spree: The True History of Science Fiction. New York: Doubleday, 1973.

> This is the best history of SF currently available. It is especially strong on the early twentieth century, though less reliable as it approaches the present moment.

Bibliography

Clareson, Thomas D., ed.
Extrapolation. College of Wooster, Ohio.

> This has been the journal of the MLA
> seminar on science fiction for over fif-
> teen years. Some of the back issues are
> obtainable from the Johnson Reprint
> Corporation in New York and London.

Mullen, R. D. and Suvin, Darko
Science Fiction Studies. Indiana State University, Terre
Haute.

> This journal was founded in 1973 and is
> currently attracting some of the finest
> SF criticism from Europe and the United
> States, including spirited debates on dis-
> puted issues in SF.

A list of titles of science fiction for the uninitiated.

> The following list is taken from works
> published over the past two decades. It
> names those Hugo, Nebula, and Interna-
> tional Fantasy award winning novels
> which I can personally vouch for as ex-
> cellent. A list of my personal favorites
> could be much longer, but by allowing
> only my negative judgments to work on
> the set of award winners I hope to offer
> the reader something more useful than
> one man's preferences. And this, too, is
> only a place to start.

1951 George R. Stewart   *Earth Abides*

1954 Theodore Sturgeon   *More Than Human*

Bibliography

1959	James Blish	*A Case of Conscience*
1961	Walter M. Miller, Jr.	*A Canticle for Leibowitz*
1963	Philip K. Dick	*The Man in the High Castle*
1965	Fritz Lieber	*The Wanderer*
1966	Frank Herbert	*Dune*
1967	Samuel R. Delaney	*Babel 17*
	Daniel Keyes	*Flowers for Algernon*
1969	John Brunner	*Stand on Zanzibar*
1970	Ursula K. Le Guin	*The Left Hand of Darkness*

Index

Aldiss, Brian, 63
Asimov, Isaac, 79
Arcadia, 59

Bacon, Sir Francis, 39
Balzac, Honoré de, 4, 14
Barth, John, 8, 69
Barthes, Roland, 4
Bellow, Saul, 22
Bennett, Arnold, 6
Best Articles and Stories,
 55
*Best from Fantasy and
 Science Fiction,* 54
Billion Year Spree, 63
Brunner, John, 72-74, 78,
 79
Buchan, John, 68
Burgess, Anthony, 23, 71,
 79

A Canticle for Leibowitz,
 60

Capote, Truman, 10
Carlyle, Thomas, 34
Charly, 55
Children of Violence, 23
A Clockwork Orange, 23,
 71
Clarke, Arthur C., 79
Coleridge, S. T., 46
College English, 46
Commedia (Dante's), 30
Conrad, Joseph, 57
Coover, Robert, 9, 24

Darwin, Charles, 35
Dante, 30, 64, 65
Defoe, Daniel, 34
Delaney, Samuel, 79
The Dispossessed, 98, 104
Don Quixote, 62
Dos Passos, John, 73
Dreiser, Theodore, 73
Dune, 67-70
Dune Messiah, 67

Index

The Earthsea Trilogy, 81, 82, 97
Einstein, Albert, 35, 36

Fantasy and Science Fiction, 60
The Farthest Shore, 81
Faulkner, William, 59
Fifth Annual of the Year's Best Science Fiction, 55
Finnegans Wake, 59
Flaubert, Gustave, 47, 58, 59
Flowers for Algernon, 54-58, 60, 61, 71

Galileo, 36
Gass, William H., 8
Guillén, Claudio, 31
Gulliver, Lemuel, 96

The Hamlet, 59
Hassan, Ihab, 8
Heinlein, Robert A., 79
Herbert, Frank, 67, 68, 70, 78
Herodotus, 13
Huxley, Aldous, 24, 79

Ibsen, Henrik, 33
In Cold Blood, 10

James, Henry, 6, 47, 58, 59

Johnson, Samuel, 34
Joyce, James, 3, 6, 49, 59

Keyes, Daniel, 54-58, 78
Köhler, Wolfgang, 35

Last and First Men, 19, 20, 63
Lawrence, T. E., 68
The Left Hand of Darkness, 80, 87-98
Le Guin, Ursula, 79-99, 104
Lessing, Doris, 23, 24
Lévi-Strauss, Claude, 35
Lewis, C. S., 80-82, 85
Literary Cavalcade, 55
Livy, 13
The Lord of the Rings, 67
Lost in the Funhouse, 8
Love in the Ruins, 23

Mailer, Norman, 9, 10
Marivaux, Pierre Carlet de, 34
Maxwell, Clerk, 85
Miller, Walter M., 60
Moore, George, 40
More, Sir Thomas, 30, 39

National Enquirer, 21
Newman, Charles, 22
1984, 71

Orwell, George, 24, 71, 79

Penguin Books, 20
Percy, Walker, 23
Planet of Exile, 98
A Portrait of the Artist as a Young Man, 59
Pricksongs and Descants, 9
Proust, Marcel, 4

Rasselas, 34
Rostovtzeff, M. I., 13
Ryan, Michael, 24

Sahl, Mort, 17
Sartor Resartus, 34
Sartre, Jean-Paul, 17
The Seven Pillars of Wisdom, 68
Shakespeare, William, 49
The Sheep Look Up, 72, 73, 77
Shklovsky, Victor, 46
Sidney, Sir Phillip, 59
"Slow Sculpture," 51
Snow, C. P., 22
Sontag, Susan, 8
"Spotted Horses," 59
Stand on Zanzibar, 72, 77
Stapledon, Olaf, 19, 20, 21, 24, 62-67
The Starmaker, 20, 62-67, 70, 77
Steele, Sir Richard, 33
Sturgeon, Theodore, 51-53, 75, 78, 79
Susann, Jacqueline, 21

Suvin, Darko, 46
Swift, Jonathan, 30, 34, 39, 88, 96
S/Z, 4

Tacitus, 13
The Temptation of Saint Anthony, 59
Thucydides, 13
Tolkien, J. R. R., 67, 78
The Tombs of Atuan, 81
Trilling, Lionel, 62

Ulysses, 6
U.S.A., 73
Utopia, 30

Verne, Jules, 15

The Wanting Seed, 23, 71
We, 71
Wells, H. G., 6, 24, 62, 79
Wiener, Norbert, 35
Willie Master's Lonesome Wife, 8
Wittgenstein, Ludwig, 35
A Wizard of Earthsea, 81, 83
Wolfe, Tom, 9, 10
Woolf, Virginia, 6

Yeats, W. B., 40

Zamyatin, Evgeny, 71
Zelazny, Roger, 79
Zola, Emile, 14, 72, 73